J. P. Dry

Ball's Bluff or Bell Berkeley's Revenge

J. P. Dry

Ball's Bluff or Bell Berkeley's Revenge

ISBN/EAN: 9783742899798

Manufactured in Europe, USA, Canada, Australia, Japa

Cover: Foto ©Thomas Meinert / pixelio.de

Manufactured and distributed by brebook publishing software
(www.brebook.com)

J. P. Dry

Ball's Bluff or Bell Berkeley's Revenge

—OR—

BELL BERKELEY'S REVENGE.

A MILITARY DRAMA IN FIVE ACTS,

WITH ACCOMPANYING TABLEAUX.

Prepared from incidents which transpired under the author's personal
observations during the great Rebellion in the
United States of North America.

—BY—

COMRADE J. P. DRY,

R. Robbin's Post, Grand Army of the Republic, Upper Sandusky,
Ohio.

Respectfully Dedicated to the Survivors of that Ill-fated Battle Field,
Ball's Bluff.

UNION CAST.

HARRY BACON, The Spy, United States Army.
JOHN BACON, Harry's Father.
SAMUEL HANSFORD, Soldier, United States Army.
CHARLES WILFORD, Soldier, United States Army.
SALATHIEL SKIDMORE, Soldier, United States Army.
CARNER MEANS, Captain, United States Army.
MAJOR GENERAL S————, General Commanding Union Forces.
COLONEL BAKER, Commanding Detachment.
UNCLE PETE, Contraband, former Slave of Matthew Berkeley.
JANE BACON, Sister to Harry.
MARY WILFORD, Sister to Charles.
Officers, and Soldiers of the U. S. A.

CONFEDERATE CAST.

MATTHEW BERKELEY, Colonel Confederate States Army.
MARION BERKELEY, Lieutenant Confederate States Army.
GENERAL EVANS, Commanding Confederate States Army.
JOHN HARVEY, Sergeant Confederate States Army.
MRS. BERKELEY, Wife to Matthew.
BELL BERKELEY, Confederate Scout and Daughter of Matthew.
Officers and Soldiers C. S. A., Ladies for Tableaux.

COSTUME—UNION.

HARRY BACON—First, citizen's dress; second, private U. S. A.; third, Major C. S. A.; fourth, rags; fifth, Captain U. S. A.

JOHN BACON—Citizen, (evening costume); second, mourning; also worn in last act.

SAMUEL HANSFORD—First, citizen's dress; second, Sergeant U. S. A.; third, Captain U. S. A.

SALATHIEL SKIDMORE—First, citizen's dress with umbrella; second, grotesque Militia Captain; third, Corporal U. S. A.

CARNER MEANS—Captain U. S. A.

GENERAL S——
COLONEL BAKER, } Army regulations 1861, U. S. A.
STAFF OFFICERS,

PRIVATE SOLDIERS—Army blue 1861.

UNCLE PETE—First, servant; second, cast-off blue; third, servant; fourth, stylish outfit at pleasure.

JANE BACON—First, afternoon dress; second, change at pleasure; third, mourning.

MARY WILFORD—First, evening dress; second, change at pleasure; third, mourning.

LADIES FOR TABLEAUX—After style required in this drama.

———

CONFEDERATES:

MATTHEW BERKELEY—First, citizen's dress; second, Colonel C. S. A.

MARION BERKELEY—First, citizen's dress; second, Lieutenant C. S. A.

GENERAL EVANS—Brigadier General C. S. A.

JOHN HARVEY—Sergeant C. S. A.

MRS. BERKELEY—Evening dress, at pleasure.

BELL BERKELEY—First, afternoon dress; second, gray riding habit; third, deep mourning.

OFFICERS AND SOLDIERS—C. S. A. 1861.

BALL'S BLUFF,

—OR—

Bell Berkeley's Revenge.

ACT I. SCENE I.

Time, April 17, 1861. *Place, London County, Virginia, home of Matthew Berkeley—Parlor neatly furnished—Characters required in act, Matthew Berkeley, Marion Berkeley, Bell Berkeley, Mrs. Berkeley, Jane Bacon, Harry Bacon and Uncle Pete.—Positions: Matthew Berkeley, C., Bell L., Marion R., two chairs R., two L., table C. with bell.*

MARION B. Father, do you think that Virginia will pass an ordinance of secession as it is called?

MATT. B. I believe that she will. I am only too anxious for the formal separation from the Union.

MARION B. I believe if the first families—and ours dates to the first colony—would take it into hand, we could force Virginia out of the "so called Union." I am sure the Bacon's will agree with us. Eh, Bell!

BELL B. I know that Harry Bacon loves his State as dearly as we do, and whatever Virginia does, you can rest assured that he will be found in a conscientious discharge of duty. But, I prize him too highly to think for a single moment that he will be found lukewarm. Roger A. Pryor has justly said to the people of South Carolina, "Strike a blow. The very moment that blod is shed, Virginia will make common cause with her sisters of the South." I can only add, if Harry Bacon can not make "common cause" with his brothers of the South, he shall never be regarded as a friend of the Berkeley's

MATT. B. Nobly spoken, my daughter! Nobly spoken! Harry is a noble young man, one whom I love next to Marion. I have long looked for the day when you, Bell—

Enter MRS. BERKELEY L. *and sits* R.

Mother did you say this morning that Harry and Jane Bacon were coming here this afternoon?

MRS. B. I must refer you to Bell.

BELL B. Yes father, Harry and Jane are coming this afternoon. We are to plan a picnic. Let me see, there will be Charles Wilford and Mary, and—

MARION B. Harry!

BELL B. I do wish that you would let me finish.

MARION B. If no one else goes I can not see who will take care of Jane. I noticed *you* quite monopolized Harry last night at Hansford's.

BELL B. Do make that pest stop teasing me.

MRS. B. Why, Bell, he has said nothing to hurt your feelings, besides you had a right to monopolize Harry. I am sure his visit this afternoon is not so much to you as it is to father and me.

MATT. B. Heyday! Are they that far along?

BELL B. Now father listen—

MATT B. [*Interrupting.*] Oh, well, he has my consent already.

MARION B. [*Rising and taking Bell's hand.*] Allow me to congratulate you. [*Sits* R.]

BELL B. Father I will not remain any longer. You have no right to anticipate. [*Goes* R.]

MRS. B. [*Rising and detaining Bell.*] Harry told me last night at Hansford's party that he would call this afternoon in company with his sister. He intimated that he wished to see father and me alone. I readily guessed what it was about. [*Placing arm around Bell.*] Nay, do not blush Bell, I know of no young man that I would sooner trust my darling daughter with than Harry Bacon.

MARION B. Well sis, how about your picnic?

BELL B. Marion, can't you hold your tongue? Yes, my dear parents I told Harry that he might call this afternoon and consult with you in regard to our marriage, but I did not think that you would anticipate. However, I feel proud to know that you approve of my choice.

MATT. B. My dear daughter, the parent would be blind indeed if he failed to see the many qualities he possesses. I am as proud of your choice as you are yourself. Marion, ring the bell. [*Rings—pause.*] Ring again. [*Rings—another pause.*] I wonder why Uncle Pete don't come.

Enter PETE, L.

Tell Sam to take charge of Harry Bacon's team when he comes. Look sharp Uncle Pete, and anticipate Harry's every wish.

PETE. [*Bowing.*] Yes sah, but Harry and Jane is gwine for to walk. [*Aside to Bell.*] Lord, Miss Bell, is Massa Harry gwine for to come? He allus gib dis poor darkey a fip or a lebby.

BELL B. Yes, Uncle Pete, I want you to earn it too. Remember what father said.

PETE. Let dis darky 'lone for dat. [*Aside, L.*] I wonder what makes Massa Harry come ober so often. Miss Bell say 'cause Harry and young Massa Marion was off to de 'cadamy togedder, but I guess its de young

MATT. B. Uncle Pete, did you hear me?

PETE. [*Starting from his reverie.*] Yes sah, I's gwine for to go.

MARION B. Uncle Pete order Neptune to be brought around immediately. [*Exit* R.]

PETE. Yes sah. Don't be in a hurry. Nep's all right.

MATT. B. [*Taking Pete by the ear.*] Go along you black rascal, do as I bid you. When the Richmond papers come, bring them up.

PETE. [*Trying to get away.*] Yes sah, I's just gwine for to go.

[*Exit* L.]

MRS. B. [*Calling.*] Uncle Pete!

PETE. [*Returning cautiously.*] Misses, Massa hurt dis darkey's ear.

MRS. B. Never mind your ear, but when Harry and Jane come show them up without delay.

PETE. Let dis darkey 'lone for dat now. [*Exit hastily rubbing ear.*]

MRS. B. I wonder what will be the result of the bombardment and evacuation of Fort Sumpter?

MATT. B. Today is the 17th day of April. Three days ago Anderson evacuated the Fort. If *I*—as an old Virginian—understand the natures of my fellow men, we can count on Virginia as belonging to the Confederacy. I am sure that Virginia will be the eighth State.

MRS. B. Father, do you think there will be any fighting?

BELL. B. Fighting, mother! How ridiculous. You know that the Northern people are nothing more or less than plebeians.

MATT. B. I see mother that Bell has the spirit of the Berkeleys in her. Don't you think she would make a good rebel?

MRS. B. If there must be any fighting, I would like for Marion——

BELL B. Why, mother, Marion could whip a dozen of those north-mudsills.

Enter UNCLE PETE, *bowing in* HARRY *and* JANE, L.

PETE. Walk in, Massa Harry, walk right in! Massa are expectin' you on bery 'portant business. Missus she tell him——

MATT. B. [*Taking Pete by the ear and leading him off* L.] You impudent black rascal, if you dare show your face in this room again I'll break every bone in your body. How are you, Harry?

General hand shaking, and seats as follows, while Harry speaks. Matt. C., Mrs. B., L. C., Harry, L., Uncle Pete, extreme L., standing, Jane, R. C., Bell, R., vacant chair at extreme R.

HARRY. Very well. [*To Uncle Pete.*] No horse today, but here's a fip. [*Hands money.*]

PETE. [*Grinning and looking at money.*] I t'ought he'd come down.

[*Exit* L.]

BELL B. We were just talking about the probable fate of Virginia!

JANE. After last night's party I would think you would not allow your thoughts to stray away with the "probable fate of Virginia." I presumed that you would be too weary to give it even a thought.

BELL B. Why Jane, we loyal Virginians feel very anxious about the
position that the mother of hospitality and Presidents may take in this
struggle.

HARRY. Spoken like all loyal ladies everywhere.

JANE. Harry is very much excited over the convention today.

Enter PETE *with paper.*

PETE. Massa here is de Richmond *Whig.* [*Sits and reads Paper.*]

MATT. Hand it here you black rascal. [*Takes paper and reads.*]

.PETE. [*Going extreme L.*] I wonder what is de matter wid Massa
today? He's awful cross. Now he's tickled, I guess he'll not break
dese bones now.

HARRY. [*Aside to Mrs. B.*] Mrs. Berkeley, do you think it prudent
to approach Mr. Berkeley now?

MRS. B. Oh yes, he has already consented.

PETE. [*Aside.*] I wonder if Massa Harry didn't come to see Missus.
I mus watch dat game and let ole Massa know.

BELL. [*Rises with Jane and going over to Harry.*] Come Harry, let
us take a stroll through the lawn.

HARRY. With pleasure ladies, I am only too proud to be your
servant.

PETE. [*Aside.*] Why in de debble don't he take Missus 'long.

MATT. Glorious news, Harry. Hip, Hip, Hurrah! Virginia now
stands as eighth State in that glorious galaxy of stars that shall battle
for freedom.

HARRY. Mr. Berkeley, I do not understand your language.

All seated as before.

PETE. [*Aside.*] Dat's what I say.

MATT. My language is plain enough, Virginia has severed the supposed chain which bound her to the Federal Union. She has—as the
mudsills would say—seceded, and joined the Confederacy. Colonel Lee
will now resign his commission in the United States service. Lieutenant Jackson will give his support to the movement, and who knows
but you may be a Major General in the Confederate army.

HARRY. Mr. Berkeley, never.

MATT. You must have more confidence in your ability. In my
opinion you were always too modest. You have an excellent education.
You have wealth and influence, and I see nothing in Harry Bacon's
way but that he can be a Colonel to start with.

HARRY. Mr. Berkeley you have mistaken my modesty and confidence in my ability, I am simply a citizen of the United States. I shall
not hesitate to fill any position that circumstances may force upon me.
My duty to my country is in my opinion, next to the duty I owe to my
God!

MATT. [*Angrily.*] A citizen of the United States! My dear sir, you
are a citizen of the Confederate States of America.

Enter MARION, R., *shakes hands with* HARRY.

MARION. Hallo, Harry, my dear boy, I am glad to see you. [*Sits* R.] Father, I see you have the *Whig*, what is the news?

MATT. Virginia has declared herself free. I fear I do not understand Harry.

BELL. Father, I can answer for Harry! He will be found in a conscientious discharge of duty. I now commission him to bring me the skull of the first Yankee he may condescend to kill. I want to make a pincushion out of it.

HARRY. Miss Berkeley you have made a grand mistake. I can not see the necessity of Virginia going out of the Union. Her rights as a Sovereign State has never been interfered with. Her citizens have no cause whatever for forcing her out of the Union.

MARION. Harry, I did not expect you to talk that way! I expected you would be true to your State.

JANE. Harry is true to the Union. He *never* will be a rebel.

HARRY. Sister, Marion only spoke in jest.

BELL. Mr. Bacon, Marion did not speak in jest. If you cannot understand Marion or father perhaps you may understand me. I now see that you do not look with favor upon a poor down trodden people. These northern yankees have imposed upon us long enough. Marion Berkeley will be found battling for the Confederacy, and you will remain home in luxury.

HARRY. Miss Berkeley, I never expected to hear such language from *you*. You forget the dignity of a lady when you stoop——

JANE. Brother, can't *you* keep quiet? Remember that in a few days or weeks you and darling Bell——

BELL. He may understand *me* first as well as last. My hand only goes to a brave noble man who can battle for the Confederacy.

HARRY. Can I believe my ears? Bell, what is the matter? I understood you to say "we loyal Virginians." I presumed you would be true to your word and not give a helping hand to sever this Union of States.

PETE. [*Fidgeting.*] Lord, dere is gwine to be a row. Jist look at ole Massa, he's mad as de debble. Look out bones.

MATT. [*Rising and advancing to Harry.*] Mr. Bacon, I presume we understand each other now!

HARRY. [*Rises.*] What I said I meant. I do not see the necessity of Virginia——

MATT. [*Interrupting.*] I care not what you see. The facts are simply these. Are you going to remain with us, or go over to that infernal crew of the North? Will you fight for your native State?

MARION. Father, be calm. Remember Harry and Jane are our invited guests.

HARRY. Mr. and Mrs. Berkeley, when I first entered here this afternoon, I felt confident that you would remain true to the old flag. That you would not urge any one to fire or trample upon its glorious folds. I am now aware that you will throw your influence——

MARION. [*Interrupting.*] Father, I would not suffer anyone to use such language. No, not even from Harry Bacon. Never forgetting for a single minute the supposed position he held to our family.

BELL. I scorn to bring to recollection, that I ever allowed *you*, Harry Bacon, to sue for my hand.

HARRY. And I am sorry that you thought that I might be a rebel.

MATT. Harry Bacon, you have used an excellent expression. Call to memory that your ancestor—Nathaniel Bacon—was proscribed a traitor, a rebel if you please. What more could we expect from a young upstart in the Bacon family?

HARRY. Mr. Berkeley, your language is ill-timed. When Sir William Berkeley was Governor of the Colony of Virginia, elected by the House of Burgess, he took sides against the colonists. My ancestor was called into the field to protect the homes of the people against native invasion. Your ancestor proclaimed him a traitor. But who was the traitor, Sir William Berkeley or Nathaniel Bacon? Any school boy can answer that.

MARION. Harry, you forget yourself. I take the liberty of telling you that your presence is not needed.

·BELL. And I take this opportunity of returning this, which I was foolish enough to regard as an engagement ring. [*Returns ring.*]

JANE. Oh, Bell, why are you angry?

PETE. [*Aside.*] De debble is gwine for to pay, so look out bones.

BELL. [*Excitedly.*] Hereafter, Harry Bacon——

MRS. B. [*Pacifically.* Bell do not be——

MARION. [*Authoritatively.*] Uncle Pete, show this northern mudsill out.

PETE. [*Running from one to the other.*] Yes sah, which one first?

MATT. [*Angrily.*] Never let me see your insolent face again.

HARRY. Sister get your wraps on and meet me at the gate. [*Exit. Jane, L.*] Mr. Berkeley, I will obey your orders. I will never enter your house as your guest. If you wish to meet me, seek me on the field of battle.

BELL. [*Sneeringly.*] If you will be as good as your word, I expect to see you on an old critter, as an aid to some ignorant Yankee.

BARRY. Miss Berkeley you have repeatedly tried to insult me this afternoon——

MARION. Harry, will you leave, or must I use force?

HARRY. Bell, I'll try and forget all you have said.

BELL. Harry Bacon, your path lies with the northern yankees; mine with the confederates. You dared insult my father in his own house. Allow me to say at parting, that you will regret every word spoken, and will bow like a slave to his master imploring my mercy. I now swear, "If I ever meet you—no matter if you were starving—I would add more fuel to the fire of your misery." Beware! Beware!!

HARRY. Bell Berkeley, bow to you! Never, no never, so help me God!"

MARION. Uncle Pete, kick him out.

PETE. [*Running from one to the other.*] Yes sah, which one fust? [*Aside.*] Massa Harry got in de hornet's nest suah.

HARRY. Mr. Berkeley, allow me one more——

MARION. Aren't you through? Remember, you are in the presence of ladies.

HARRY. [*Goes L.*] Ah, yes, I do remember your sister is here!

MATT. Stop, Harry Bacon, I have one word to add before we part. Today you came here as an invited guest, and the accepted suitor of my daughter's hand. You now leave this house with the eternal curses of each of its inmates resting upon your head. As my daughter has said, you will live to see the day that you will bow to, and implore the the mercy of the Berkeleys. I now simply add that Uncle Pete will show you out, hoping that I may never more see your hated form.

HARRY. I will admit, Mr. Berkeley, that this is your house; you have the right to say who shall and who shall not enter. Your threats however, fall harmless upon me. As for my bowing to you, I will repeat the language I used to your daughter, never, no never! You referred me to my ancestor and tried to point the finger of scorn in that direction. I now refer you to Nathaniel Bacon with pride, and with contempt to Sir William Berkeley who proclaimed him a traitor. I will now say, it was the Berkeleys with all their patents of nobility who bowed to the Bacons. Beware, Mr. Berkeley, that your curses may not fall upon your head or yours!

MARION. Father, why do you allow such language? I'm sure I would not in my house.

BELL. Oh, you insulting wretch! Were I a man, I would throw you out of the window. No doubt when you and your yankee crew invade our sacred soil you will take pleasure in waging war upon defenceless women and children. But hark, Harry Bacon! Though a woman, my time, yes, my undivided time, will be given to the Confederacy! When you hear of the doings of Bell Berkeley you may well tremble. I now swear eternal vengeance upon the whole northern fanatic crew. Yes, Harry Bacon, you will be sorry you ever crossed the path of a Berkeley!

HARRY. Miss Berkeley, I believe you are transformed into a fiend. I feel proud that I am free of you.

BELL. No, you are not free of me. You will meet me when you will be sorry.

MATT. Your insulting language can not be indured any longer. I had not intended to enter the army, but your insolence has decided me. I will go to teach you a lesson. I sincerely hope that I may be able to meet you where you can defend yourself.

HARRY. Mr. Berkeley, you have driven me from your house with the eternal curses of each of its inmates resting upon my head. I will

say that you will find me in the Union army. You will see that you
make your words good, and not like a former Berkeley, run from a
Bacon.   [*Exit* L.]

MATT. Insulting coward, I am glad that he has left! I could only
keep from lying hands upon him from the knowledge of his being invited here.

PETE. Yes sah, Massa Berkeley, didn't I kick 'im out?

MATT. Clear out, you black rascal, or I'll break every bone in your
body.

PETE. Massa can break de bones of de poor darkey. [*Aside.*]

MATT. Stop your muttering you black imp, or I'll break every bone
in your body. [*Menancingly.*]

PETE. [*Aside.*] I t'ought he'd break de bones.

MATT. Clear out, you black rascal.

PETE. Massa I's de brest nigger——

MATT. [*Interrupting and pointing L.*] Go!

PETE. [*Going L. Aside.*] Look out for dis darkey. Yes sah, I's
gwine for to go.   [*Exit* L.]

MRS. B. I can hardly believe my senses. A peaceful party broken
up, and the Bacons who were once our friends are now our enemies.

BELL. Mother, do you regret it? I feel proud that I am free as my
native hills. Any man who can join the yankee army and battle against
his native state, should never be recognized as a southern man. Father,
you and Marion must enter the Confederate army. I would advise that
you raise a regiment, and *I* will be adopted as its daughter.

MARION. No, sister, nothing that savors of yankeeism will be toler-
ated. There will be no such thing as a daughter of the regiment in the
Confederate army.

BELL. I can do better. I can go as a scout for our noble cause.
[*Cheers off left.*] Hark! [*Looking left.*] Ah, look father, the people
are wild with excitement. [*Clear stage and*

[CHANGE.]

SCENE II.

*Street in first grooves—Citizens run on Singing Dixie—at end of song
all exit and*

[CHANGE.]

SCENE III.

Tableau—Secession—Slow curtain.

END ACT I.

ACT II. SCENE I

First grooves—Time, April 17, 1861—Place, London County, Virginia— Home of John Bacon—Parlor neatly furnished—Characters, John Bacon, an old man; Harry Bacon, his son; Jane Bacon, sister to Harry; Samuel Hansford, Charles Wilford, Salathiel Skidmore, Uncle Pete, Mary Wilford, sister to Charles; Carner Means and soldiers required through act. Positions, John Bacon, C., Harry, L., Jane, R., Chairs R. and L.

JOHN B. So my dear boy, Matthew Berkeley had the impudence to call you a traitor? You whom I taught to look upon that glorious ensign of liberty as resembling the rising sun. These fire-eaters are trying to trample it in the dust. Oh, Harry, had I been there Matthew Berkeley and that spirited Bell would have received their own.

JANE. Father, I think your absence was a God-send. Harry heroically defended the name and dignity of the Bacons.

HARRY. Father and sister let us dismiss this disagreeable subject. Virginia has passed an ordinance of secession. We who are true to the Union are in danger of our lives. We must cast our lot with the North ; and he who dares stand back, or give aid to this secession movement, or "fire upon that dear old flag, should be shot down upon the spot." By the way, father, Samuel Hansford, Salathiel Skidmore and Charles Wilford will be here this evening.

JOHN B. Have you in any way ascertained the position they may take in this coming struggle for national existence ?

JANE. Charles and Samuel whom we met in the grove as we came home grew rather excited over the movement. To know that their ancestors were hung without being allowed the privilege of bidding their friends good bye, by the orders of that tyrant, William Berkeley, in the dark and gloomy days of the Colony of Virginia, is sufficient evidence that they will be true to the Union.

JOHN B. True, daughter, I should never have doubted them for a single moment. I understand that our neighbor, Mr. Means, has said that in case this movement must be settled by the stern arbitration of the sword, he would give his undivided time to the Union cause. I think my boy, that you and I will see him tomorrow and urge him to raise a company of men, and John and Harry Bacon will head the list.

HARRY. Oh, father, take into consideration your delicate health. You can not endure the fatigue of the march and battle. Father I im-

plore you by the sacred memory of my departed mother, your affection-
ate companion of your youth, stay at home and take care of sister.
Your age will be a sufficient safe-guard to you while I am away battling
for our country. No one can doubt your loyalty to your country under
circumstances like these. When duty to my poor distracted country has
called me away from those who are near and dear to me, pray that
the Great Jehovah who presides over the destinies of men, may watch
over and protect us in the army! Should it be necessary that our lives
should be placed upon the alter of our country, that we should be so prepared to meet him in His Celestial abode where war and rumors of war
are heard no more forever.

JOHN B. Harry, Harry my noble boy! Where is the parent who
could not be proud of such a son? Harry, your action—your language
has instilled into me the sacred thought that the spirit of your
dear departed mother is looking down upon us tonight with an angel's
approval. [*Rising.*] Go my dear boy (*placing hand on head,*) and may
Heaven's choicest blessing be yours while you are battling for freedom
against the enemies of our land. I now humbly pray (*rises eyes and
hands upward,*) that He who watches over us, will bring you back safe
when this struggle is over.

JANE B. Amen! [*Stage illuminates and Mrs. Bacon appears at
back as an angel, looking on approvingly.*] My dear brother, our parting will be very, very sad. Oh, Harry, how can I give you up? [*Clings
to Harry.*]

HARRY. Come, dearest sister, do not grieve so. My country calls for
my aid. I must obey. There, now dry those tears. [*Knocking* L.]
Sister our friends are at the door. [*Both go* L.]

Enter UNCLE PETE, SAM HANSFORD, CHAS. WILFORD, SALATHIEL
SKIDMORE *and* MARY WILFORD. PETE *steps quickly to* C. *and intro-
duces them.*

PETE. Massa Bacon, and Massa Harry, I has de berry insignificant
honor ob interducing de right honorable gentlemen ob de—ob de—why,
Miss Jane how does yer do?

General greeting and seats as follows: JOHN B., C., JANE, SAMUEL
and CHARLES, R., HARRY, MARY, SALATHEL *and* PETE, L.

HARRY. Uncle Pete, can you enlighten us why we have the great
pleasure of your ever welcome company, after what happened at your
master's today?

PETE. Well you see, Massa Harry, dat ole Massa ob mine he sent me
for to see who all was gwine for to fight for de Souf; and says he, "Pete
you black rascal, keep an eye on dat start-up, Bacon, and 'port de 'sult
at de earliest 'wenience. I tells you Massa Harry, if I is brack I haint
forgot all de fips and lebbys, nor de cuffs and kicks. I puts de kindness
of de Bacons in de one side ob de balance, and 'buse in de udder. De
'buse goes 'way up, and de kindness down. So I's here to help you all.

Massa Berkeley he don't need for to tink I's gwine for to play de spy and 'port de 'sult.

JANE. I will answer for Uncle Pete. He has long looked on a change as being necessary for his welfare.

PETE. Now Miss Jane, don't say any more. All dis fine talk will spile dis darkey. I is simply Pete if I is brack.

CHAS. No more need be said on either side. Uncle Pete is true blue.

PETE. I isn't blue I tell yer, I's brack.

SAM. Mr. Bacon, we came over to consult you in relation to our bleeding country.

JOHN B. My dear friends, the action today of some of the would be leaders, has taken the noble State of Virginia out of the Federal Union. I feel sorry that my native State is thus ruthlessly torn from that Union of States, in which she was first to enter in the dark and bloody days of '76. "But let them lift the hand of parricide in the insolence of pride, or madness of power, to strike their country, and her countenance in all the severity and terror of a parents wrath shall smite them with amazement and horror. Let them strike, and the voices of millions of freemen from the city and the hamlet, from the college and the farm house, from the cabin amid the western wilds, and our ships scattered around the world, shall utter the stern irrevocable judgment, self-banishment for life, or ignominious death. The Union is to us the marriage band of States; indissoluble in life, to be dissolved we trust only on that day when nations shall die in a moment never to rise again" My dear friends that union which was formed at the price of blood shall be maintained at the price of blood; and by the aid of the Great Jehovah we will be one and inseparable. Virginia is the eighth star ruthlessly torn from that galaxy of stars which formed the grandest constellation of stars the world ever knew. We today should stand before the world, not as a single state, but as a united mass—which should be north and south—willing to chastise the rebellious spirit engendered by the doctrines of Calhoun. We should not at this moment stand back and allow rebels—for such we must now call them—take any undue advantage. We must strike, one and all, for one grand purpose, to suppress one of the greatest rebellions that ever entered the minds of fanatics upon this or any continent. It will be carried on with fire and sword. I expect to be houseless before forty-eight hours roll over my head, because I am found true to my country. Matthew Berkeley will head a gang of men to meet out summary vengeance upon my noble boy who dared tell him that this Union was inseparable. I repeat that by the aid of all loyal people it will be inseparable. Each United States volunteer will stand ready to yield his life if necessary for the restoration of this Union.

PETE. [*Aside.*] I wonder what ole Massa Berkeley would say or for to do if he heard dat now. Old Massa Bacons' a brick. [*Puts on Sala-thial's hat.*]

SAL. [*Rising with umbrella in left hand.*] Mr. Bacon, I expects that I'll pull my ole sword out'en the scabbard tomorrer and muster my

men. I've just been and wanted ter tell you all as how my men is all
dyin' for a fight. I'll grind up that 'ere old blade and march into 'em
right and left.

PETE. Is dat so?

SAL. We havn't done anything since John Brown was hung.
[*Swings umbrella.*]

PETE. Dat's what we heard you say.

MARY. Salathiel, please be seated. You did excellent service then
in London county while John Brown was being hung over in Charles-
ton, about thirty miles from here.

SAL. [*Seated.*] Well, wasn't I held in reserve? I know'd that this
war was a comin' and I'd be ready. [*Brandishes umbrella and hits Pete
who is trying to dodge his movements.*] I expects you all will look sick
when I plucks this 'ere "secession goose" tomorrer, and you'ns has done
nothing at all.

JANE. Yes, Salathiel, when you have accomplished all your fancy
paints, we will be sorry. You had better devote your time in the re-
cruiting service. You, will no doubt be promoted to a high privacy in
the rear rank.

PETE. Pri-hivacy, what's dat now? You allus talks in niggermas.

JANE. Salathiel will tell you.

SAL. Well, Uncle Pete, in the first place——

PETE. Dat's what you say. [*Hitching chair.*]

SAL. There will be low privates in front ranks——

PETE. Yes sah.

SAL. And there must be high——

PETE. Dat's what you said. [*Continued hitching at chair.*]

SAL. And I am going——

PETE. Why don't you go den?

SAL. Let me finish. Where was I? What was it I said?

PETE. Exactly.

SAL. Oh yes, I'm going to the rear——

PETE. In course you is and nebber stops till de battle obber.

SAL. [*Discovers his hat on Pete's head. Speaking with much dignity.*]
See here you black rascal——

PETE. Exactly, I's lookin'.

SAL. [*Rising and stepping to Uncle Pete who retreats* R.] Take that
hat off your infernal black cocoanut or I'll——

PETE. Exactly, you'll go to de rear. [*Drops hat.*]

Salathiel picks up hat, Uncle Pete goes L. *and sits on Salathiel's chair.
Salathiel bows to the ladies, and retires backward and sits in Pete's
lap, who throws him on the floor. Mr. Bacon assists Salathiel to rise,
and points to chair extreme* L. *which Pete resumes.*

JANE. Uncle Pete, I believe you and Salathiel understand going to
the rear.

PETE. Now, Miss Jane, I had to go and for to show de boy de way it was done. But Massr Harry, what's de use foolin' de ebenin' away dis way?

HARRY. Thank you Uncle Pete, for the reminder. Well boys will you go with me in the morning to see Mr. Means? Let us be his first.

OMNES. Agreed!

SAL. (*Rising and brandishing umbrella*.) I'll muster my company and march down before you all are out of bed.

MARY. How many can you muster?

SAL. [*Sits reflecting—counts on fingers—puts on hat—places umbrella under chair. Pete takes umbrella and hoists it*.] Let me see ; about seventyfive.

OMNES. Seventyfive!

SAL. Well, there are seven——

MARY. [*Interrupting*.] Seven! As many as that?

SAL. I think I could raise five——

PETE. [*Chuckling and interrupting*.] You might raise five umbrellas.

CHAS. W. Uncle Pete you are always welcome, but you had better go home. Mr. Berkeley might break your bones.

PETE. Massa Charley, I's not gwine to tell all I knows.

CHAS. W. You know Uncle Pete, your bones have so often been broken by Old Berkeley, that you should not incur his displasure.

PETE. 'Cur! What's dat now? Is it a dog?

JOHN. B. No, Uncle Pete, we think your Master might get angry with you for staying with us this evening.

PETE. [*Aside*.] I knows where de shoe pinches. [*To Mr. Bacon*.] Massa Billy, he say I's true blue. All I's got for to say or for to do I's true black! Massa Bacon can't you buy me and let me go 'long wid Massa Harry to de wars?

JOHN B. I guess not. But you could go any way.

HARRY. How much did your Master say you were worth.

PETE. He said if I was old he could sell me for two hundred dollars.

HARRY. As you are the bone over which there will be——

PETE. [*Interrupting*.] Who's a bone?

HARRY. You.

PETE. You go 'long, I's no bone.

HARRY. You are a two hundred dollar bone, and one of the causes of this war.

PETE. I's done noffin. What has I done?

HARRY. You do not comprehend . Uncle Pete you are not worth a cent.

PETE. [*Crestfallen*.] Not worf a cent?

HARRY. I believe that is what I said.

PETE. Massa Harry, I allust' ought you a mighty fine man ; but you for to go for to say dat I's not worf a cent, is more dan I can bear. [*Wringing hands and letting umbrella fall*.] Massa Harry I's de brest darkey my old Massa has!

CHAS. W. Uncle-Pete you do not understand Harry.

PETE. [*Not heeding.*] My God, what a fall de niggers hab had in a few minutes.

HARRY. Uncle Pete, today you are free; Virginia is the eighth State that has passed, and all the remaining slave holding States will pass ordinances of secession. It will only be a question of time when the shackles will fall from the feet of the African slave in the United States of North America. If I were you, at the first opportunity I'd go to some Federal Camp.

PETE. Dat's a sorrel horse wid a brack color. Golly, Massa Harry. what'd old Massa say or for to do if he'd cotch me?

SAM. H. Go with us in the morning, we'll take care of you.

PETE. Is I worf nothing?

SAM. H. You will be to us in camp; you can cook, etc.

PETE. I can't and-so-forth. I's done forget how.

SAL. Uncle Pete, you can go as my servant. All officers have servants.

PETE. When you go to de rear you'll need two servants.

SAM. H. Now Uncle Pete, you go home, and tell your old Master that we are true blue, then meet us in the grove tomorrow morning.

PETE. I's gwine for to go suah! Look in dese brack orbs and say if you can see anyt'ing green dere! I isn't gwine for to play de spy on Massa Harry if he did say dat de nigar was worf noffin'. Dat was an offle tumble. I's gwine now for to widdraw from dis auturem assembly, and find dat couch on which cheap niggers can tumble and rest dere weary bones. Now I's gwine. [*Exit* L.]

SAL. I must go to. I must muster my men.

CHAS. W. Do so!

SAL. [*Rising and Sooking for Umbrella which he has in his hand.*] I do believe that infernal imp has taken my umbrella.

MARY. You have it in your hand.

SAL. I didn't mean this one. I meant the one I carries on Sundays.

[*Exit* L.]

CHAS. W. Ladies, sing "The Red, White and Blue." After which we will adjourn our little patriotic meeting.

OMNES. Yes, sing!

SAM: H. We can then enter the army and battle for freedom with the knowledge that at least there are two Virginia ladies who are anxious for our welfare.

Mary and Jane Sing "The Red, White and Blue." At the end of last verse Goddess of Liberty appears at back and points South.

[CHANGE.]

ACT II, SCENE II.

SECOND GROOVES—*Salathiel marches five men over stage from L. to R. dressed oddly, carrying old fashioned arms, bunches of hay and straw tied on feet. Salathiel front, calls hay-foot, straw-foot. Sabre in right and umbrella in left.* [*Exit* R., *slowly.*]

Enter Uncle Pete L. *cautiously, with a bundle of clothing which he carries on his shoulder.*

PETE. I wonder if de boys's come? Now I's gwine for to look around and see if anybody's watchin'. [*Looks cautiously.*] Massa Harry had for to go and for to say I's not worf a cent. Lord nigger's cheap. I couldn't sleep a bit for dat lofty fall. I's now gwine for to find dat shackle what's to fall off de niggers feet. [*Examining feet.*] I's got no shackle, I wonder if it's de shackle what de preachers reads about? I expects it's money. [*Looks at feet again.*] No money dere. I 'spose its de long point on de nigger's foot. [*Examines heel.*] If dat's it den dis nigger can wear a number lebben wid ease. I wonder if de white folks hain't got de shackles chopped off when dey's a pic-a-ninny? Well dat shackle is a niggerma to dis poor darky any way you fix 'er up. I's gwine to sit down and wait for de boys. [*Sits.*] I wonder whose bones old Massa will break since I's worf nofin'. Dat fall from two hundred dollars to noffin took de bref from dis poor old darky and break de shins too. Hallo dere comes de boys.

Enter boys L.

CHAS. W. Uncle Pete, what is in this bundle.
PETE. Dat's all de worldly possessions ob dis poor darky. Old Massa Berkeley he sent me ober dis mornin' to play de spy on Massa Harry, so I's here to cook and-so-fort' for you boys.
CHAS. W. Let us go. We have fooled too much time already.
[*Exit* R.]
PETE. Well old Loudon county, I gibs you one long last lingering gaze. [*Exit.* R.]

[CHANGE.]

ACT II, SCENE III.

THIRD GROOVES—*Exterior of Mr. Mean's house—Mr. Means seated L. at table—paper, pens and ink on table—Head resting on right hand —soliloquizing.*

MEANS. Alas! Virginia thou hast taken a step in this secession movement which will require the lives of your best citizens! Not only those who in their blind fanaticism think it a duty; but those who were taught from infancy to look upon this Federal compact as being inseperable. "The greater the interest, and the more sacred the rights which may be at stake, the more absolutely should we appeal to the generous feelings, the noble sentiment, the calm, considerate wisdom which become a free, educated, peaceful, christian people. The Union is the property of the world, no less than of ourselves; that it is a part of the Divine scheme for the moral government of the Earth, as the solar system is a part of the mechanism of the Heavens; that is destined while traveling from the Atlantic to the Pacific, like the ascending sun, to shed its glorious influence backward on the states of Europe and forward on the empires of Asia." Edmund Ruffin, an old intimate friend of Calhoun, has in his old days committed a blunder, which fired the native Virginian to a revolution which will——. Ah, who comes here? [*Takes chair L. front.*]

Enter Salathiel with squad, calling hay-foot, straw-foot—Marches slowly L.— Countermarches—Then left flank—Halts.

SAL. Well boys, you'ens done well. Now we is at Mr. Means' house, I expects ye to hold yer heads up, look peert, and don't fergit the commands, and I'll make officers outen you all. [*Put down saber and takes umbrella in right hand.*] Now boys, I'll go inter the house. [*Discovers Mr. Means L.*] Hallo General, we wants to 'list.

MEANS. Very well. Your name is Salathiel Skidmore I believe.

SAL. S. [*Proudly.*] Some folks call me Salathiel; but my true name is Mr. Captain Salathiel Skidmore, Esq.

MEANS. Is that all? Why not continue your name "*ad infinitum.*"

SAL. To please you I'll "*ad infinitum.*" Well General, what is the involution you want done?

MEANS. Have them number from right to left.

SAL. Boys, number from left to right. Be right smart. [*The boys pull out cards on which the numbers one, two, three, four and five are printed respectively, in large figures, which they pin on coats.*] General, look at that now. [*Brandishing umbrella.*]

MEANS. Do you mean your sword?

SAL.. [*Looks at umbrella—aside.*] He'll think I'm not military.

MEANS. [*Pointing at cards.*] Where did you get those cards?

SAL. You told me to have them number from left to right. They is obedient, so they puts the numbers on the coats so they won't forget it.

MEANS. [*Pointing to feet of squad.*] What is this hay and straw for?

SAL. Why you see when we marches, we all steps off with the same foot.

MEANS. Which foot do you step off with?

SAL. With the hay foot of course.

MEANS. [*scrutenizing.*] Which is the hay-foot?

SAL. Can't you see it is the left foot.

MEANS. Why, here are three with the hay on the right foot.

SAL. That is fixed for a retreat. [*About faces the three with the hay*

on their right feet.] Now, you see General, it is on the left foot.
[*Proudly.*] Oh, my army is obedient! [*Throws down saber and picks my umbrella.*]

MEANS. What do you want with that umbrella?

SAL. [*Aside.*] Cuss that umbrella, I thought it was the sword. [*Exchanging umbrella for sword, and addressing Means.*] I thought you'd want it to keep the sun off.

MEANS. No, no! Have your men number in twos.

SAL. Boys, number in twos, be right smart now. [*Each one calls two.* That was good, what next?

MEANS. Have them go through te manuel of arms.

SAL. Go through 'Manuel's arms? Oh, yes! 'Manuel come here. [*First one comes to Sal.*] Boys put down your guns. [*They ground arms.*] Now 'Manuel put your arms togeher. [*Emanuel does so.*] No, no, this way! [*Forms circle and Emanuel imitates.*] Now hold on to that 'ere persish. Sam, come here. [*Sam advances.*] Go through 'Manuel's arms, head first. [*Tries to force Sam. through Emanuel's arms.*]

MEANS. No, no! Boys, take up your arms. [*They do so and reform line.*] Order arms! Shoulder arms! Present arms! [*Squad rush to Captain and hand their guns to him.*] No boys, Salathiel is your drill-master!

SAL. In course I is. You see General, they allers obeys orders. I was goin' so show you a involution in 'Manuel's arms.

MEANS. I see they are obedient. Have them mark time by file left.

SAL. How lucky! [*Produces large file and takes up saber.*] Now boys, pull out your little books and pencils and mark the time it'll take me to file this old blade. [*Goes to the left of stage front, calling as he draws file harshly over saber,*] you'ns mark time, I'll file left.

MEANS. [*Interrupting.*] What are you doing?

SAL. Why, I'm filing this ere old blade while they are marking the time it takes me! Oh, we is doing jist as you ordered!

MEANS. I see that this is one of your "new involutions."

SAL. In course it is! [*Picks up umbrella.*] What next?

MEANS. Have them pass in review.

SAL. Have them pass in review? I'll be blamed if that ain't lucky, I happen to have this 'ere Review in my pocket. [*Produces large newspaper.*] Now boys, when I holds this 'ere paper up to your noses, you say pass as we do when we play euchre. [*Salathiel holds paper to each ones face and they say pass.*] Now that was good! You see, General, we understand all the involutions. We was drilled when John Brown was hung, we was! What next?

MEANS. Have them double up.

SAL. [*Very solemnly.*] Now boys, I wants you'ens to double up. [*Extends number one's feet and puts number two's head between them.*]

MEANS. What are you doing?

SAL. (*Men resume natural positions.*) Having them double up.

That's a fine movement, that is! My men is well drilled. I tells yer
General, I drilled them myself when old Brown was hung. What
next?

MEANS.   I want to ask you a few questions.

SAL.   Ask away.

MEANS.   What do you expect to be if you enter the army?

SAL.   I am already Mr. Captain Salathiel Skidmore, Esquire Junior "ad infinitum." If I goes inter the army I expects to be Mr. Captain
Brigadier General Salathiel Skidmore, Esquire Junior "ad infinitum,"
in the United States Army?

MEANS.   If you enter my company I will give you an important position.

SAL.   Name that 'ere important position.

MEANS.   Eighth corporal.

SAL.   Eight corporals!

MEANS.   Will you go?

SAL.   I'll take that offer into consideration.

MEANS.   Very well, now march your men to the house. (*Marches
to L. U. E. where squad exits, Salathiel looks for them.*

Enter Harry, Pete and others R.—Salathiel runs against Pete.

PETE.   What you go for to run agin me for? You tink nigger's
cheap!

SAL.   I'm lookin' for my army.

PETE.   Dey's gwine to de rear. Massa Harry, is dat de shackles you
talk about? (*Pointing to Salathiel's feet.*)

SAL.   You go 'long, you doesn't know anything about war.

PETE.   Is dat hay and straw to feed de brack horse cavalry?

SAL.   (*angrily.*) You go 'long, I'm lookin' for my army.

PETE.   (*laughing.*) Get some grass, you'd find 'em sooner.

HARRY.   Uncle Pete, recollect you are on probation.

PETE.   I ain't on 'bation, I'm on dese ere scows.

MEANS.   (*shaking hands.*) I see that I'll have no difficulty in organ-
izing a company of independent men for the war.

Enter John B., Jane B. and Mary W.   Cordial greeting.

JOHN B.   Mr. Means, will you organize a company of loyal Virginians for the suppression of this rebellion? If not, I'll see what I can do.

MEANS.   Mr. Bacon, your delicate health, to say nothing about your
age, should tell you that this work should be left to those who are
younger. I have fully made up my mind that this war will last for
years. Therefore, we need the services of all able bodied men, not those
like yourself, who are willing but not able. I can not doubt your patriotism for a single moment. To know that Harry will go is to be in-
ferred by his presence with these boys whom I regard too worthy to
meet the fanatic crew who will oppose us.

PETE.   Massa Means, Massa Harry shook up all de Berkeleys——

HARRY. Uncle Pete, you must be quiet. Yes Mr. Means, our mission this morning is to see you. While some of us may be called to yield his life in defense of his country, we hope that we may never regret the step to be taken by us today. Your remarks to father are in substance what I have heretofore told him.

MEANS. We will then proceed at once.

HARRY. Boys sign that roll, while I talk to father.

All sign except Salathial.

JOHN. Harry, my noble boy, its hard to give you up. Why can't I go too ?

HARRY. Father, your duty is at home with my darling sister. Mine where my country directs.

JANE. Father, I feel confident that Harry will return to us. Oh father, do all in your power to encourage the noble boys who are willing to battle for our distracted country.

JOHN B. My darling children, I'll do everything in my power. Go, Harry, sign that roll. When the war is over return to us again. Your father and sister will ever pray for your safe return. Let no action of yours during your term of service ever tarnish the name of Bacon. That name stands high in the history of our country. .It is to be perpetuated through you. Go, boy, go !

JANE. Harry, your sister's prayers will ever guard you. When temptation may beset your foot-steps think about our sainted mother, up there.

HARRY. God being my helper, I will. (*Signs roll.*)

MARY. (*Coming to Jane.*) I feel so sad to think that our associates are to be deprived of home and its comforts, probably for years.

JANE. I feel the same way.

HARRY. (*Coming front.*) Father, what I have done I hope I may never regret. I have only done what you would have done if your age and bodily infirmity had not prevented.

JOHN. (*Addressing the boys.*) Harry, and your associates, allow me to say, that what you did any true patriot should have done. Remember that the soldier and gentleman are combined ! To you, Mr. Means, I entrust the welfare of these noble men. I expect to hear that in a conscientious discharge of duty, your little command will strike terror to the hearts of the blattant rebels of Virginia.

MEANS. Mr. Bacon, I accept the charge of those noble Virginians. Boys, go to the house, you'll find suitable uniforms. (*Exit boys, L.*)

JOHN. Salathiel, why do you fool with hay and straw on your feet ? Your country calls you, will you go ?

PETE. He wants de hay to feed de calves.

SAL. Dry up you black imp, or I'll——

PETE. (*Interrupting.*) I's a free niggar. I got a two hudred dollar fall last night. I tell yer Salathiel de white folks what carries de umbrella is as good as de nigger ?

MARY. Go Salathiel, sign that roll, I will go with you and give you that encouragement that only a woman can give where her country is in danger. (*Salathiel signs roll and exits with Jane.*)

PETE. Massa Means, can't I—that is, can't I—

MEANS. Can't I what?

PETE. Can't I go for to be a soger boy?

MEANS. Uncle Pete, you are a slave, I have no right to take you. The President has said that the "peculiar institution of slavery shall not be interfered with, providing the South will remain in the "Union."

JOHN. African slavery will be wiped out of the United States through this rebellion. I shall this day execute and deliver to each of my servants freedom papers. Uncle Pete belongs to a man who drove my children from his house because they dared speak in defiance of him for the Federal Union.

MEANS. Well, Uncle Pete, Mr. Bacon has won the day for you. You may go with us. (*Going.*)

PETE. I wants to 'list like de boys.

MEANS. Certainly, come and sign the roll. (*Hands pen.*)

PETE. Massa Means, now you—that is—I got the rheumatiz in de left eye, and I can't hold de pen good.

MEANS. You spell your name, I'll write it.

PETE. Spell dat name? You's foolen' wid me now. My mouf was' spiled eaten' de hoe cake when I's pick-a-ninny. But I'd spell dat name if I had no mouf at all.

JOHN B. Go on Uncle Pete, spell your name.

PETE. My name is Pete. I's gwine to spell it suah. You see I's one ob de spellers, I is. So, here goes: F. F. V.

MEANS. Correct, you are now one of the boys and an F. F. V.

JOHN B. Uncle Pete!

PETE. I's here.

JOHN B. You must be obedient to the captain and a father to the boys.

PETE. Let dis darkey alone for dat. When I cooks de and-so-forth, I'll gib de "and" to de boys and keep de "so forth" myself.

MEANS. Let us retire, no doubt Berkeley has his spies watching.

JOHN B. We have just captured one of his spies in the person of Uncle Pete.

PETE. Now, Massa Bacon, you knows I's no pie-cake or bread. I's a free darkey gwine for to be a soger boy.

MEANS. All right. Let us go. (*Exit L.*)

PETE. Now white folks look out, I's a "fleet-footed Virginian."

(CHANGE.)

Enter Bell Berkeley R., Cautiously.

BELL. Yes, Harry Bacon, I've watched you closeley. Little did you think when you signed that roll that Bell Berkeley was near. You will regret your action, and as I said yesterday, bow to me. Revenge, revenge thou art sweet! I will never rest until you are in my power; and then haughty, proud, Harry Bacon beware, beware!

SCENE V.

THIRD GROOVES—*March music, company enters. After marching around stage for star, then form line at rear of stage. Samuel H. O. Sergt. Charles W. Sergt, Salathiel Corporal. Enter ladies with colors L first entrance.*

JOHN. B. Captain, I see my daughter wishes to speak to your command.

CAPTAIN M. Attention! Shoulder Arms!

JANE B. (*Coming forward to Captain M. with colors.*) Captain Means, in behalf of my friends, allow me to present to you this emblem of liberty which our forefathers secured at the cost of thousands of lives during the long and bloody days of the revolution; whose lives were given to the Union, which is today threatened by a rebellion, which nothing but the strong arbitration of the sword may subvert. I entrust it to your care and keeping, and when in battle, when the rebel hordes shall fire upon it, remember that He who watches over us all, and protects us by His care will ask at your hands to keep it unsullied. May you rally around it, and strike terror in the hearts of a relentless foe. When this war, this cruel, cruel war is over, return this emblem of liberty if in shreds, but with all the stars shining forth in all their splendor. May high Heaven watch over you, and care for you and your command during the dark and dreary days of this rebellion. (*Hands colors to Captain M.*)

CAPTAIN M. (*receiving colors.*) Miss Bacon I accept at your hands this ensign of liberty. I sincerely hope that I may be able to do as requested by you. Although some of us must be a sacrifice upon the alter of our country; yet we sincerely hope that we may ever be found battling for the right, and when danger besets us on every side, this emblem will instill into our minds that the fair donors expect of us to keep it unsullied. Ladies, I thank you for this invaluable gift. Sergeant, four paces to the front, March! (*Charles Wilford advances.*) I entrust you with this sacred emblem (*hands* CHAS. W. *colors*) and expect you to keep it unsullied as long as life may last. Sergeant, when we are battling for our country, let your thoughts revert back to this occasion with pride at being selected for this honorable position. When we have earned an honorable discharge, and this rebellion suppressed return it to these fair donors, who will ever pray for our success and the safety of this emblem of which you now have the honor of protecting with your life! By the aid of all loyal soldiers we will not lose a single star, but return this emblem of National liberty with each and every star as firmly fixed upon it, as each star is fixed in the starry firmament up there! Present Arms! Shoulder Arms! Post March! I now propose three cheers for the fair

donors of this beautiful stand of colors, (*cheers*) Fix bayonets! Stack
Arms! You now have a few minutes to talk to your friends.   Break
ranks, March !

(General handshaking.)

HARRY B.   Father and sister, *(taking each by the hand,)* though we
are seperated for a time perhaps never to meet again, be true to your
country and your God !

JANE B.   Oh, darling brother, I can never forget your last words.
Remember that your good name is at stake.   Oh, Harry, Harry, I can
not give you up! *(clings to him and weeps on shoulder.)*

HARRY.   Sister I must not be unmanned now.   Dry these tears.
When I return home we can then talk about the happiness in store for
us. Good by darling sister. *(goes to Mary.)* Mary remember me
kindly when I am away. Yesterday, by blind infatuation I imagined I
loved a woman whom I thought worthy. Today the scales have fallen
from my eyes, and I not only see her unworthiness but find that I have
made a very narrow escape. I feel that a union with her would be
filled with such a loathesomeness that life itself would have been a burden.   I now caution you against her, watch over my sister, and try to
avert all threatening danger that may beset you through that family.

MARY W.   Your manly open way has called forth my better nature.
I shall ever cherish your confidence at parting. Oh, how proud I am
of you and Charles.   Be as brothers to each other while in service for
your country.

CAPTAIN M.   Attention! *(rank reformed,)* Take arms! Unfix bay-
onet! Shoulder Arms! Right face! Music! Forward march! *(march
around stage and at R. C. E. exeunt.)*

*Samuel H. and Jane B. L. Harry B. and Mary W. R. John B. and
Charles W. C. Tableau of parting, stage illumines and Mrs. Berkeley
appears as Angel, Slow music, Slow curtain.*

ACT III, SCENE I.

THIRD GROGVES—*Headquarters of General S.   General S. and staff
seated around table examining maps.*

COLONEL.   It is my opinion General that the rebel force is vastly superior to ours in point of numbers. As this is an avenue to Maryland
we cannot leave it ungarded, I believe Jackson is in command.

COLONEL S.   It may be. I feel confident however that General
Evans is the commanding officer. But as to the size of his command I
am unable to tell.   Colonel, have Captain Means report here immediately! Captain tell Colonel Baker to report forthwith ! *(exeunt Colonel
and A. D. C. R. and L.)* I must ascertain all the particulars. The de-
partment expects that I dislodge the enemy at once. I will entrust this
dangerous expedition to Colonel Baker *(enter Captain M. saluting Gen-*

eral S.) Captain have you a man in your company in whom you have implicit confidence? One whom you could recommend for his truthfulness and daring? One who could not hesitate to undertake a mission where honor awaits if successful?

CAPT. General I have.

GENERAL. Have him report to me immediately. (*Captain salutes and exits L.*) If I am not disappointed in that man I can ascertain all I want for Colonel Baker's success. Ah, here is Colonel Baker! (*Enter Colonel Baker L.*) Colonel I sent for you on important business, I am ordered to dislodge the Confederate force on the Upper Potomac. I find a small force concentrated on the opposite side of the river. You will take two regiments of infantry, a section of artillery, and Captain Mean's Company of Independent Virginians who have been converted into a company of cavalry. Here are your orders regulating your movements. [*handing orders.*] You will hold yourself in readiness to move tomorrow morning.

COLONEL. General have you ascertained anything definite in regard to the enemy's strength, position, etc.?

GENERAL. I will send a man from Captain Mean's Company, who formerly lived close to Leesburg for that purpose, and have him report his observations to you.

COLONEL. I will be ready to move at a moment's notice.

GENERAL. Do so. [*Exit Colonel Baker L. after saluting General.*] I hope the expedition will be a success. [*Enter Harry Bacon L. who stands at attention, and when recognized by General salutes and hands orders.*] Soldier, Captain Means sends you here with his compliments. Can you comprehend why?

HARRY. No sir!

GENERAL. We are about to attack the enemy at Leesburg. We have no knowledge of his force. It would be madness to attack him without first ascertaining something definite in regard to strength and position. I will not ask you to undertake the mission until you fully understand its responsibilities. If you accept, you are to penetrate the enemy's lines, ascertain his strength, position, and who is in command. If you are successful, promotion and honor await you. If unsuccessful and detected, the awful doom of a spy is yours! Do you fully comprehend the mission?

HARRY. General, I fully comprehend the mission.

GENERAL. Will you accept it, knowing its consequences?

HARRY. For the benefit of my country General I will accept the mission knowing the consequences.

GENERAL. Soldier, you will procure the necessary disguise and penetrate the lines immediately, and return as soon as possible and report the result of your observations to Colonel Baker, who will have the command of the expedition. I will only add that you must be cautious. You are a native Virginian and no doubt will meet those who were once your associates and neighbors. [*Harry salutes General and Exit L.*]

I can now take a few minutes rest.

SCENE II.

FIRST GROOVES—*Enter* L. *Marion Berkeley with a detachment of Confederates, Marion as Lieut.*

MARION. Halt! Front face! Right dress! Sergeant Harvey you will take the detachment to yon bluff. (*pointing* R.) I will expect you to hold the position until further orders. The bluff commands the road to the river, and we expect an attack from that point.

SERGEANT. Will I report any movement of the enemy?

MARION. No, I'll come up soon.

SERGEANT. Attention! Right face! Forward march! [*Exeunt* R.]

Enter Uncle Pete L. *cautiously.*

MARION. What are you doing so far away from town?

PETE. Misses she sent me to see de General.

MARION. What General.

PETE. Why the Confederate General ob course.

MARION. General Evans?

PETE. Dats de feller. He come often to see my misses.

MARION. If you talk that way about General Evans, I'll tell Mrs. Carnes.

PETE. [*going* R. *aside.*] Young Massa Marion don't know dis darky.

MARION. You are on the wrong road to see the general. [*goes up to him.*]

PETE. [*trying to get away.*] I's just gwine down de road. I's coming back soon.

MARION. [*detaining him.*] You cannot go down that way, our pickets are on the bluff.

PETE. Yes sah, I's just done gone suah. [*Aside.*] De pickets on de bluff. Dis nigger's not blind.   [*Exit* L.]

MARION. If I had not sent him back, General Evans would have lost an invitation to tea. Mrs. Carnes is true to our cause and a widow!

MATTHEW. [*enters from* L. *as Col. C. S. A.*] As I anticipated General Evans I ordered Sergeant Harvey to go with you. Here is an order.

MARION. [*opens and reads.*] "Headquarters Confederate forces Leesburg Va.   October 20, 1861.

SPECIAL ORDER No. 27.

Lieutenant Marion Berkeley will report to these Headquarters forthwith. He will be designated as Provost Marshal and have his office close to these Headquarters.

By Command of Brigadier General Evans.

F. C. BARNS, A. A. A. G."

I am now able to attract the attention of the authorities and my promotion will follow.

MATTHEW. Yes, but your sister now outranks you, she has just been handed a Major's Commission, and is assigned to the secret service.

MARION. For heaven's sake you did not give your consent? Well father we must now go back to Headquarters. [*Exeunt* L.]

SCENE III.

THIRD GROOVES—*Confederate forces in line. Enter General Evans and staff. Forces saluting. Enter Matthew and Marion B. saluting General E.*

MARION. General, in obedience to this order, I am at your service.

GENERAL. To whom did you leave the command of the pickets on the bluff?

MATTHEW. Sergeant John Harvey, I'll be responsible for him.

GENERAL. Colonel, you will give it your personal supervision. If an attack is made it will be at that point. You will see that Sergeant Harvey has proper instructions. Double his force, and hold that point at all hazards!

Enter Harry Bacon R, as Major C. S. A.

HARRY. [*Saluting General Evans, and handing him orders.*] General Jackson sends compliments, and respectfully asks that you give these documents your immediate attention.

GENERAL, [*reading.*] "General Evans, I send herewith by Major Carson—My A. D. C.—this order, and hope that you will treat him with all the courtsey due his rank. T. J. JACKSON, Major General." ·

"Headquarters Confederate forces in the field near Strasburg Va., October 20, 1861.

SPECIAL ORDER NO. 14.

BRIGADIER GENERAL EVANS Commanding Confederate Forces Leesburg, Va..

You will report by letter and entrust it to my courier—Major Carson—the strength of your command and position. You will also detach three regiments of infantry to join me at Winchester without delay. Any negligence may prove fatal to the cause in which our lives, our fortunes and our honors are at stake.

T. J. JACKSON, Maj. Gen'l. C. S. A.

[*calling.*] Colonel, send three regiments immediately to join General Jackson at Winchester. They will subsist upon the country they march through. [*Exit Col.* L.] Hand that abstract [*to aid*] to Major Carson that the adjutant prepared this morning, showing the number of men fit for duty. [*Exit aid* L.] By the way Major, I have recommended a young lady who is noted for her daring and attachment to our cause for a Major's Commission. My recommendation has been acted upon and today I have handed to Bell Berkeley————

HARRY. Bell Berkeley?

GENERAL. Yes Major, do you know her?

HARRY. Bell Berkeley, no I believe I never heard the name.

GENERAL. [*Turning to Matthew.*] Colonel Berkeley, allow me to introduce to you Major Carson of General Jackson's staff.

COLONEL. [*Salutes and shakes hands.*] Major Carson I am always glad to meet a fellow soldier.

HARRY. Thank you. [*Aside.*] Oh heaven give me strength, I did not expect to meet *him* here !

Enter A. D. C. with abstract and detail for three regiments.

AID. General, by your permission I will hand the abstract to Major Carson.

GENERAL. Do so. [*converses apart with officers.*]

AID. Major here is the necessary information. [*Handing abstract.*]

HARRY. Thank you. [*Aside.*] Colonel Baker instead of Jackson.

Enter L. Uncle Pete.

PETE. [*takes off hat and bows.*] Misses she sent me for to tell you dat she wants you for to come to tea. [*Aside.*] Massa Harry here and dressed like de rebels !

GENERAL. Tell her, that Miss Berkeley and Major Carson will be there with me.

PETE. Yes sah. [*Aside.*] Dat poor boy has gwine for to change his name. Oh lord, what'll poor old Massa Bacon say ?

HARRY. Uncle Pete, don't recognize me.

PETE. [*Aside to Harry.*] So you isn't Major Carson.

HARRY. [*Aside to Pete.*] In heaven's name don't let old Berkeley or Bell recognize you or we are both lost !

PETE. [*Aside to Harry.*] Let dis darky alone for dat. [*to General Evans.*] General Evans is you gwine for to come ?

GENERAL. Oh yes, we'll be there.

Enter Bell B. L. dressed in gray riding habit showing rank of Major on left lapel.

BELL. General, has papa come back ?

HARRY. [*Aside.*] Must I meet her too ?

GENERAL. [*to Bell.*] Oh yes, Major Berkeley, Major Carson of General Jackson's staff. [*Introducing.*]

BELL. [*Extending hand.*] Major Carson I am happy to meet you.

HARRY. [*acknowledging introduction and releasing hand.*] Thank you. The General informs me that your devotion to our cause prompted him to recommend you for a commission in our army, I hope that you may be able to instill into the hearts of our noble men such heroism, that we may at all times hurl back those yankee invaders from our soil !

BELL. Thank you for the compliment. [*courtising.*] I can only do my duty to a people who are oppressed by a horde of yankee invaders !

GENERAL. Major Berkeley, I will leave Major Carson in your care. We are expected to tea at Mrs. Carnes this evening. General Jackson has so completely crippled me in case of an attack that our army will be taxed to its utmost, and defeat stares me in the face. But let us go.

[*Goes L.*]

BELL. Come Major (*to Harry.*) General Evans has placed you under my care. (*Takes Harry's arm and crossed from* R. *to* L.) General Evans, father, I have detected treason in our camp!

OMNES. Treason!

GENERAL. What?

MATTHEW. Treason! Where?

PETE. (*Aside.*) Massa Harry's gwine up suah.

BELL. (*disengaging arm.*) Here in the person of Major Carson!

HARRY. (*aside to Pete handing papers.*) These papers! Colonel Baker! Hurry.

PETE. (*aside to Harry.*) I's gwine for to go suah!

GENERAL. Major Carson what is wrong?

BELL. Look father! All! (*removes disguise.*) Behold Harry Bacon! (chord.)

HARRY. (*proudly.*) Yes Bell Berkeley, behold Harry Bacon!

MATTHEW. Harry Bacon I expected to meet you where you could defend yourself.

HARRY. I ask nothing at your hands.

BELL. Harry Bacon where is your boasted patriotism?

HARRY. I am in your power do your worst.

GENERAL. We are wasting valuable time. (*to aid.*) Captain, countermand the order for the detachment of those three regiments immediately. (*Converses with chief of staff.*)

BELL. Do you remember how you insulted my father in his own house?

HARRY. Bell, you are determined to have revenge.

BELL. Remember my oath!

HARRY. I expect nothing from a Berkeley.

GENERAL. (*to Matthew B.*) Colonel, are you personally acquainted with this man?

MATTHEW. Yes General, I am personally acquainted with him. He insulted me and mine when a guest. He is a member of Captain Mean's Company of renegades.

HARRY. A hard word Colonel Berkeley. Take it home. Remember our past friendship!

MATTHEW. I do remember it all. Harry Bacon remember our parting words!

HARRY. Colonel I do, I am now aware that you are heartless!

GENERAL. [*to Matthew B.*] Summon a court-martial immediately. If convicted let him suffer the doom of a spy! Colonel, I entrust the execution of the sentence to you. Come Major let us retire. [*Exit with Bell* R.]

Matthew B. summons a court-martial.

MATTHEW. Soldier, what was your object in entering our lines as a Confederate officer.

HARRY. Suffice it to say I am here as such. I will not answer your questions.

MATTHEW. Soldier, do not be too hasty. If I were to use my influence with General Evans I could induce him to mittigate your sentence. If a position were offered in our service——

HARRY. Do you think for a single moment that I could so far forget myself as to turn my back upon my country in time of need? Never Colonel Berkeley! You can do your worst.

MATTHEW. Take into consideration your age, your ability, your poor and aged father——

HARRY. Colonel Berkeley, remember by your actions he was made homeless. Never refer to my father again. Do you suppose that I would be a traitor to my country. My comrades and my father for the sake of life given in such a way? Do you think that I could be so base as to bring my father's gray hairs with sorrow to the grave? Call to memory the simple fact that I am a Bacon! Now do your worst.

MATTHEW. Yes I remember that you are a Bacon. I also remember that you are a Virginian as well. Will you give up your foolish idea?

HARRY. Once and for all, no. I am a soldier of the United States!

MATTHEW. Harry Bacon, do not I beseech you be too hasty in your conclusions. Can you not be induced——

HARRY. Call to memory Colonel Berkeley, the time when you and your family were friends in whom I took pride to recognize. Take into consideration the time when you drove me from your house with the eternal curses of each of its inmates resting upon my head. Now when death stares me in the face, you ask me to be a traitor to my parentage and my country to save a life which in after years would be like Benedict Arnold's. No, Colonel I am in your power, and the execution of the sentence which no doubt will be a pleasure to you can not be executed too soon. I would rather die a thousand deaths than have the finger of scorn pointed at me, and have it said that through fear and by the persuasion of rebels I——

MATTHEW. Enough! Officers what is your verdict?

OMNES. Death to the spy!

MATTHEW. Harry Bacon, I am sorry that you are doomed to an ignominious death! (to officer.) You will see that the sentence is immediately and properly executed.

OFFICER. (to Harry.) Soldier I am commissioned to perform a duty which will launch you from time to eternity. Do you really consider the enormity of the condition in which you are placed?

HARRY. Yes I have really considered it, I have no regrets, and have but one favor to ask. If you ever meet my father—John Bacon—or perhaps you may meet my sister, tell her that I met my fate as a brave man!

OFFICER. Soldier, I will conduct you to your position. (*Dead march, advance to* L. *meet Matthew B. who extends hand. Harry refuses to recognize him, then* L. *to* C. *officer bandages eyes. Harry kneels to commune. Adieus with officer.*) Attention! (*Guard forms.*) Make ready! Aim! ——

BELL. (*rushing in from* L.) Stop!

MATTHEW. Why daughter what is wrong?

BELL. Harry Bacon is my prisoner as you will see by reading this order. (*hands order to Matthew.*)

MATTHEW. (*examines order.*) I see that Harry Bacon's execution is indefinitely postponed. Bell take charge of your prisoner.

BELL, (*removing bandage.*) Well my dear Harry Bacon, you will never bow to a Berkeley. Thank Bell Berkeley for saving your life.

HARRY. I would prefer death a thousand times than ask life at your hands.

BELL. You will be more humble after while. Father dispatch a sergeant to relieve Sergeant Harvey, and have him report to General Evan's headquarters without delay. (*Exit* L. *with Harry.*)

SCENE IV.

FIRST GROOVES—*Enter* R. *Colonel Baker reading papers, met* C. *by Harry B.*

COLONEL. I see by these papers you sent with a colored man that the enemy's original number has been reduced.

HARRY. The order for detachment when I was detected was immediately countermanded. We must now contend against their combined forces.

COLONEL. I now apprehend danger. The river is now between us and General Stone's remaining forces.

HARRY. I will only suggest that as we are in their hands, we sell our lives as dearly as possible.

COLONEL. Report to Captain Means for duty. After the battle report to my headquarters. [*shaking hands.*] Good by. God only knows what a day may bring forth.

Skirmishing L. *Federal soldiers cross from* R. *to* L. *enter aid from* L. *and salutes Colonel Baker.*

AID. The rebels are on our front with their full force. Major Ashton was killed at the first volley. I am fearful Colonel the tide is against us.

COLONEL. Tell Captain Means to advance his company to the support of the skirmishers and hold the enemy in check at all hazards. (*Exit aid* L.) (*examines field with glass.*) Captain send the artillery immediately to the Left. Have three companies of infantry to support the artillery. I pray heaven to give us aid, as I am fearful we are in a trap. [*Exit* L. *with Captain.*]

SCENE V.

THIRD GROOVES—*Federals driven back to right, rally and advance to
L. Driven back, rally and charge. Colonel Baker killed, Matthew
Berkeley mortally wounded, Marion Berkeley killed and Harry Bacon
wounded. Tableau. John Bacon, Jane Bacon and Mary Wilford in
attitude of prayer.*

SCENE VI.

FIRST GROOVES—*Enter Salatiel L. with umbrella in left hand.*

SALATHIEL S. Oh lord—Grand rounds again—I'm killed—I'm—Oh
why did I ever enlist—I want ter go home.—

Enter L. Uncle Pete with musket.

PETE. Salatheil wasn't that orful?

SAL. Stand back, you're another grand rounds. Stand back I say or
I'll run this umbrerella down your mouth and then h'ist it.

PETE. (*singing.*)

> "Massa was a Colonel in de rebel army
> 'Eber since he's gwine away,
> But the Yankee's got him
> And I think they've shot him
> Eber since de fust ob May.
> CHORUS. Look out dere now,
> I's gwine to shoot!
> Look out dere, don't you understand.
> Babylon is fallen, Bablyon is fallen
> And I's gwine to occupy de land."

*When Pete says "I's gwine to shoot," he brings gun up to his face and
Salatial hastily retreats R. followed by Uncle Pete.*

SCENE VII.

THIRD GROOVES—*Battle field. Music "who will care for mother now."
Harry Bacon lying R. C. Matthew Berkeley C. Marion Berkeley L.
C. Colonel Baker front C. Wounded soldiers of Union and Confederate soldiers lying promiscuously over stage. Enter R. & L. opposing
officers with flags of truce at back, meet C. shake hands, and pass
through dead and wounded. Sisters of charity on the field. Enter
Uncle Pete R. finds Harry Bacon and partially rises him up, kneeling
at Harry's side.*

PETE. Oh Massa Harry is you dead? Speak to poor old Uncle Pete.
Poor old Massa Bacon your boy is done gone.

HARRY. Father, Sister where are you? (*sister of charity advances.*)

SISTER. Can I do anything for you?

HARRY. Sister tell father not to greive for me I'll soon meet mother!

SISTER. Yes, yes, but you must not exert yourself!

PETE. De poor boy is dying!

HARRY. Water! Oh give me water!

PETE. Look up poor Massa Harry! Uncle Pete has water for you.
(*holds canteen to Harry's lips.*) Don't yer know me Massa Harry?

HARRY. Where am I? Oh this pain!

MATTHEW. Mother, Marion, Bell where are you?

HARRY. [*reviving*.] Uncle Pete raise me up. [*gazes at Matthew B.*] Colonel Berkeley we have again met!

MATTHEW. Harry Bacon, my life will be the forfeit for my rashness towards you an honored friend and guest of our family. As I expect to meet my God on that day when the grave shall give up its dead, I humbly beg your pardon, and ask you to forgive my hot-headed children. Harry——

HARRY. Mr. Berkeley, in your better days you have been a valued friend of mine. Yesterday you asked me to desert my flag when I was in danger of losing my life. Today when death is staring us both in the face you ask my pardon for your cold cruel treatment, and to forgive your hot-headed children. As God is my Judge I sincerely forgive you and Marion.

MATTHEW. [*gasping*.] And Bell.'

HARRY. She tried to crush my heart, and only had the execution of the sentence stayed yesterday for the purpose of my eking out a miserable existence at her hands. Mr. Berkeley I never can forgive the cruel taunting language of your daughter? [*falls back.*]

MATTHEW. Oh Harry—in—the—name—of our—past—friend—ship —[*dies.*] [*Confederate officer finds report of forces on Colonel Baker's person.*]

Enter Bell Berkeley and John Harvey L. 1st E.

CONFED. OF. [*handing paper to Bell.*] Here is a report of our forces found on the body of this yankee Colonel.

BELL. [*examines report.*] The same that Harry Bacon obtained yesterday.

SERG'T. HARVEY. [*discovering Marion.*] Bell, Miss Berkeley here is Marion and dead!

BELL. [*kneeling over him.*] Oh darling brother you were compelled to yield up your young life for your country! [*to confederate soldiers.*] Soldiers, bear him yonder (*points L.*) and let us give him a christian burial. Oh, Marion, Marion, my only brother gone! [*wringing hands and staggers back to where Matthew Berkeley lies.*] Oh father, can it be possible that you too are dead? [*kneeling over him.*] Father, father, speak to me! Don't you hear your darling daughters voice? Can it be possible that I am bereft of both a father and a brother! Yes Harry Bacon you once said "Beware that your curses do not fall upon your head or yours." My burden is greater than I can bear. [*sinks to the ground. Soldiers bear off Matthew B. L.*]

HARRY. Sister!

SISTER. What can I do for you?

HARRY. Where is Uncle Pete?

PETE. Here I is, Don't you know me Massa Harry?

HARRY. Yes I know you and recollect all. Raise me up. There that will do. Uncle Pete if I never get well tell father that Matthew

Berkeley begged my pardon, and wanted me to forgive his daughter before he died !

BELL. (*rousing up.*) So Harry Bacon we have met again ! Yesterday you dashed me to the ground, and made your escape only to fall into my hands now. Yonder (*pointing L.*) lies a dear father and an only brother riddled by your cursed yankee bullets, and I only am left of that proud family to break the sad, sad news to my mother ! Sergeant Harvey, take this man in charge, and when you have faithfully discharged your duty by torture and starvation—when Harry Bacon will bow to you and me, like a dirty dog that he is, come to me and claim your bride !

SERGEANT. The only boon I could ask. Your instructions will be carried out to the letter.

HARRY. So Miss Berkeley you could even torture a wounded man to gain your revenge. Take my life now but do not allow Uncle Pete to carry the sad news to father and sister that—

BELL. Uncle Pete, *how do you do ?*

PETE. I hain't got time, I's got to take dat umbreller out ob my mouf.

BELL. *My dear old Uncle* step this way.

PETE. I tells yer I hain't got time, I must cook de and so forth for de boys.

BELL. Lay that nasty carcas down.

PETE. How often must I tell yer I hain't got time.

HARRY. [*Aside to Pete.*] Get away from here. Get word to father that Bell Berkeley has me in her power.

PETE. [*Aside.*] Let dis darkey alone for dat. Dey don't need for to tink I's altogedder green if I is brack.   [*Exit* R.]

BELL. Pete, did you understand me ?

PETE. [*outside.*] I tell yer I understands, but Miss Bell I wants yer to understand I's a free nigger and not worf a cent. Jist take one long last lingering gaze at de bone of secession for I's off for de ribber.

BELL. Stop that darkey. I must have him. He is one of our slaves. [*soldier goes R. after Pete.*] Sergeant Harvey there is your prisoner. I will see General Evans and get you properly detached for this special duty. Spare no means to make his captivity as unbearable as possible. Remember that I through him have lost an honored father and a dear brother. By a strict obedience to orders you win a wife.

HARRY. Miss Berkeley in your better days you would not stoop to talk to John Harvey. Why do you commission him to torture me ! Am I to be tormented by you and your confederate in crime ? I cannot help but think that you are possessed by an infernal fiend. John Harvey poor miserable wretch that he is, is a fit tool for you !

SERG'T. [*raising gun to strike.*] One word more and your life will be the forfeit !

HARRY. Strike, insolent coward ! Death is preferable to the misery that you are capable of heaping upon me.

BELL. [*staying Harvey.*] Hold, I desire torture only!

HARRY. You are capable of anything.

BELL. Look upon my father and brother whom your insolence forced into the army, and find an excuse for my actions!

HARRY. Excuse! How did you taunt me when at your house by your insolence? Call to memory the epithets hurled upon my head. Oh Bell, you are a fiend, a double——

SERG'T. Do you suppose I can be a silent spectator and listen to your insolent language addressed to my affianced? [*takes hold of Harry.*] Get up and take a last look at your surviving comrades for I swear you shall never see them more.

Takes Harry off L. Stage clear. Tableau. Colonel Baker with crown, with two little girls dressed in white as angels, one on each side. Heavy light, slow curtain.

END ACT III.

ACT IV. SCENE I.

FIRST GROOVES—*Front of Libby Prison Richmond, Virginia. Time Nov. 1861.*

SERG'T. [*coming from L. with H.*] My letter of instructions settles all disputes as to whom you belong. [*sneeringly.*] Your dear Bell Berkeley will be my bride when you are sufficiently tortured, I gain a bride you once coveted, one who would not speak to me before this war as you said the other day. [*tauntingly.*] How times, manners, and customs change. Eh my fine bird?

HARRY. Could I provoke you sufficiently insolent wretch, I would thank you for taking a life that God gave me. Yes taunting coward strike your victim!

SERG'T. Very complimentary. Hear this order. [*reads.*]

"Headquarters Confederate forces)
Leesburg, Va., October 22, 1861.)

SPECIAL ORDER, No. 29.

Sergeant John Harvey of Company A Second Virginia Infantry C. S. A. is hereby detached from his regiment and will immediately report to Major Bell Berkeley of the secret service

By Command of Brigadier General Evans.

F. C. BARNS, A. A. A. G."

Now give me your undivided attention "my dear fellow" while I read your dear Bell Berkeley's letter of instructions, [*reads.*]

"Office of Secret Service)
Leesburg, Va., October 22, 1861.)

Sergeant John Harvey of the Confederate army has in charge one Harry Bacon who was detected by me in our camp as a spy for the Yankee army, who was convicted and sentenced to be shot. The said John Harvey is to keep this said Harry Bacon in solitary confinement in or about the city of Richmond, in the state of Virginia, reserve sole control, starve, torture and otherwise abuse him as in his judgement may best suit my interests.

BELL BERKELEY, Major Secret Service
C. S. A."

You can rest assured that her instructions will be carried out to the very letter!

HARRY. Fiend! Miscreant! Wretch! Leave me or I'll not be responsible for what I may do in my frenzy!

SERG'T. Remember Harry Bacon [*drawing revolver.*] I'm not to be trifled with.

HARRY. Shoot fiend! I would rather be shot than tortured to death!

SERG'T. No Bacon, I'll not kill you my orders are different.

HARRY. Insulting wretch and fit tool for Bell Berkeley I cannot provoke you sufficiently to perform a deed of mercy by taking my life! Well here I am to be placed in solitary confinement and father and sister ignorant of my fate. I find that Bell Berkeley belongs to the secret service and no doubt sought and gloried in the position, while I more unfortunate was detected in obeying my superior officer and condemned to death! I would rather die from an honest conviction of right than be starved and tortured to death!

SERG'T. Come along, you have said enough. Here is Libby Prison your future home. (*forcing Harry off R.*)

SCENE II.

THIRD GROOVES—*Home of John Bacon. Parlor neatly furnished. John Bacon R. C. Jane Bacon L. Mary Wilford R. Uncle Pete L. C. Seated C.*

PETE. As just said, I helped dat boy out ob jail at Harrisonburg, and the rebels got him back. He's now in Richmond, but Massa Bacon if you says so I'll make one more effort.

JOHN B. It is useless. Aid cannot reach him now. Let us hope that he will be exchanged.

JANE. Poor hope indeed.

PETE. Well dis poor darkey has done all he could.

JANE. We do not censure you. We feel confident that you did all you could for Harry.

MARY W. Mr. Bacon, I sympathize with you. If he never returns life will be a blank to me.

JOHN B. I fully appreciate your feelings for my dear boy. We may probably never see him until this "cruel war is over."

Mary sings "When this cruel war is over" and at last verse Harry appears at back in tableau in prisoners garb. Heavy light, slow curtain.

SCENE III.

FIRST GROOVES—*Time, March, 1865—Enter Sergeant John Harvey reading order, L.*

SERG'T. "Sergeant John Harvey will take his prisoner—Harry Bacon—to Belle Island, where I will meet him to confer what will be the best mode of disposing of him.

BELL BERKELEY, Major Secret Service
C. S. A."

So you'll be here will you? You have not made your appearance for a long time. You will not recognize him, whom you so madly loved before the war. What do I care whether she recognizes him or not so I can secure the Berkeley estate. I have labored long and hard, and almost sold my soul to the devil for the consumation of my wishes, but don't seem any closer than when I first began. You used to point the finger of scorn at me, but become my bride, and damn me if I don't point the finger of scorn the other way. [*Exit* R.]

SCENE IV.

THIRD GROOVES—*Belle Island. Time, April* 1865, *same day that General Deven entered Richmond. Prisoners in rags, scattered promiscuously over stage.*

HARRY. Yesterday, for the first time I was allowed to hold intercourse with my fellow prisoners. I have been in Libby Prison, Castle Thunder, Tobacco Ware house and on this Island over three years! I receive daily barely sufficient food to sustain life. Harvey has done his work well. Bell Berkeley you deserve such cruel treatment as I have passed through, and you will receive it at the hands of John Harvey when you become his wife! Oh I am so hungry! I wish I had what the dogs receive at home! The dog which was choked and eaten yesterday on this island was more palatable than the filth which we receive daily, and for that action we are to be deprived of food for days to come! We must have bread!

PRISONERS. Bread! Bread! Bread! (*walking aimlessly over stage.*)

Enter R. Serg't Harvey with guard.

SERG'T. See here yanks, (*drawing knife*) "If any one opens his head again I'll make crow's meat out of him."

HARRY. Yes John Harvey, if this thing continues much longer you will not have any for crow's meat as you term it. The poor wretches who are here under you are so emaciated that they are not recognizable. Why am I kept here? Why am I not exchanged? Yes John Harvey you have played your part well! You will soon win your bride! Bell Berkeley——

SERG'T. (*rushing on Harry with knife.*) Take that you insolent scamp. Never allow the name of Bell Berkeley to cross your lips again.

HARRY. Coward, why not strike home? You can do a deed of mercy by ending this life by one thrust of your dagger.

SERG'T. You are tired of life are you? When you bow to Bell Berkeley and me and ask our pardon you may be liberated.

HARRY. Bow to her, never! God being my helper I never will!

My sainted mother taught me when a child to bow to none but my
Heavenly Father! But to bow to Bell Berkeley a noted rebel I *never*
will!

SERG'T. Take care how you talk! (*raising knife.*)

HARRY. (*advancing.*) Coward! Fiend incarnate! You cannot
strike too soon!

BELL. (*entering R.*) Well sergeant I see you are faithful to orders.
You will soon receive your reward.

SERG'T. The only reward I ask is the fulfillment of your promise
made years ago on the bloody battle-field of Ball's Bluff!

BELL. I never forget a promise, or forgive an enemy. (*to Harry.*)
Well my fine fellow how do you like army life now?

HARRY. I had hoped I never more would see your hated form.
Why am I thus tortured?

BELL. Remember my oath, at my father's house, and by the side of
my dead father and brother at Leesburg who were murdered by your
cursed yankee crew! Had it not been for "your insolence" father
would be at home today. Had I—— but no Harry Bacon I *will* have
revenge!

HARRY. Why not instruct your tool there (*pointing to Harvey.*) to
end this miserable existence? Why not *you* with all your boasted chiv-
alry, either secure an exchange or give us bread! Bread! Bread! I
can endure this no longer!

PRISONERS. Bread! Bread! Bread!

SERG'T. Shut your mouths and stop your howling. You will get
bread after you have paid the penalty for the dog which disappeared!

BELL. Sergeant, you will see that my orders are carried out to the
letter. Harry Bacon when you bow to me and beg my pardon you will
be treated like the rest.

PRISONER. I can not see why any one should be treated worse than
we!

HARRY. Boys, we must have bread! Must I bow to that fiend?
(*pointing to B.*)

PRISONER. Hunger forces us to do things that our better natures
hold in disgust. The man would not be degraded.

SERG'T. Man! I see nothing but yankee dogs here.

HARRY. We were men once! You have starved us inch by inch
until every trace of manhood is gone, and now we beg for bread! Bell
Berkeley you have at last accomplished your mission. (*falls at her feet.*)

BELL. I thought you would never bow to Bell Berkeley, now wretch
beg my pardon. (*laughs.*)

HARRY. (*rising.*) Beg your pardon? Never! Give these poor boys
bread. Why should they suffer because I refuse to beg your pardon!

BELL. I now instruct the sergeant never to give you anything to eat
until you are willing to beg my pardon as well as to bow to me.

HARRY. The devil himself could not torture a human being as you
and your expectant husband——

SERG'T. Harry Bacon you have referred to Miss Berkeley with sneering insinuations long enough. (*kicks Harry until he falls.*) Take that and learn to be more circumspect in the future.

BELL. Sergeant, you fully understand orders. Well my fine fellow how do you like army life now?

HARRY. You have accomplished everything you intended to perform. Oh how humiliating to beg the pardon of a person you never wronged. We must have bread! Bell I beg your pardon for what I may have said to you.

BELL. Beg Sergeant Harvey's pardon as well.

HARRY. (*partially rising,*) The sergeant who kicked me just now? No I'll die first. He has used me like a dog.

SERG'T. You are worse than a dog! Some dogs will obey their masters, but you must be taught obediance by cruelty.

BELL. Bring in some bread, just enough to make them feel that obedience will secure more.

PRISONERS. Bread! Bread! Bread! (*crouching on the ground.*)

SERG'T. Guard bring in some bread? (*Exit guard R.*)

BELL. He is unable to rise.

SERG'T. He must be taught that we are his masters. (*enter guard with bread.*) Here is something to eat. (*Prisoners rush up.*) Stand back. (*drawing knife.*) This is all you may expect for two days unless you point out the man who——

HARRY. (*trying to rise.*) Oh give me bread! I am dying of hunger and cruel treatment. Father, Sister, Mary why do you not come? Oh mother I see you now. Your Harry will soon be there. (*falls back.*)

SERG'T. Here yanks. (*prisoners advance.*) Stand back! (*throws bread on ground.*) Help yourselves. (*prisoners quarrel over bread.*) I see Bacon will get none.

BELL. General Lee sent a dispatch to President Davis today who received it in church. What its purport is I cannot say.

SERG'T. Tomorrow I'll return and fix this fine chap. Remember your promise. Attention guard! Left face! File right! March!

[*Exeunt.*]

BELL. If Lee is forced to fall back we are in a desperate strait. "We will die in the last ditch before we surrender." Yes Harry Bacon you not only bowed to me but begged my pardon. I have had sufficient revenge upon him now. I am certain that under the treatment he has daily received he will be a fit subject for the lunatic asylum. The dashing Harry Bacon of Leesburg is a thing of the past.

HARRY. Boys have they gone and not given us bread?

PRISONER. ;Here Comrade, try and eat this. (*gives bread.*)

BELL. Whose bread are you giving away? Harry Bacon you will receive no bread from your fellow prisoners.

HARRY. Is that fiend here yet? In the name of Heaven, in the name of our past friendship end this miserable life! Go to father and

Jane and tell them that I implored you to end a life which was a burden
to me, and they will bless you.

BELL. No, Harry Bacon, remember my oath! (*Exit R.*)

PRISONER. A fiend incarnate! (*Going L.*)

GUARD. Halt! (*Shoots prisoner.*)

PRISONERS. Oh, why not me? (*Bending over dead prisoner.*)

(*Volley L., orchestra starts up "Tramp, Tramp, etc."*)

PRISONER. Tramp, tramp, the boys are maching. We are rescued,
we are free!

[*Enter Union Soldiers L. singing, "Rally Around the Flag Boys."*]

SOLDIER. Now boys, three cheer for the old flag. (*cheers.*) Lee has
fallen back. Grant is in hot pursuit. General Devans has taken pos-
session of Richmond! We are sent here to liberate you. Those who
are left of the brave boys in this prison pen are as free as the air!

PRISONERS. Thank God!

SOLDIER. Who is this poor soul? (*Pointing to Harry.*)

[*Bell Berkeley and Sergeant Harvey brought in R.*]

PRISONER. That is Harry Bacon, a native Virginian, who has been
kept in solitary confinement since the battle of Ball's Bluff, by that fiend,
(*pointing to Bell*) and tortured by that miscreant, (*pointing to Sergeant
Harvey*) who resembles a man. I am fearful that his days are num-
bered. He has just been kicked by that brute because he would not beg
his pardon. Our food was thrown upon the ground, and Harry did not
get any, nor was I allowed to share mine with him.

LIEUT. Secure these fiends and take them to General Devans' headquarters. (*Bell and Harvey are handcuffed.*) Soldier, (*to Harry*) do
you not recognize your old friends? See, the old flag waves on Belle
Island.

HARRY. What? Flag! Bell——(*mind wanders*).

LIEUT. Do you not recognize the old flag? [*Holds it over him*].

HARRY. Father! Sister! Come here! Where am I! [*Partially
rising.*] Mother, I see you now! There, don't you see her? [*Recognizes Bell.*] Take her away! Fiend, don't, don't kick me now! Boys
did I bow to her? Ha! ha!! ha!!! [*Falls back.*]

LIEUT. [*To Sergeant Harvey.*] Is this your work?

HARVEY. Yes, I have the honor of being the instrument in the
hands of Bell Berkeley of making a wreck of Harry Bacon.

LIEUT. Bell Berkeley, the noted rebel spy?

BELL. Call me what you please, but do not couple me with this poor
silly fool. [*Pointing to Harvey.*] He has unjustly punished this man,
as he has many more, contrary to orders received from the proper authorities. There is another of his victims. [*Pointing to dead soldier.*

LIEUT. [*Looking at dead soldier.*] This is indeed horrible! Can
men so far forget themselves as to butcher helpless victims?

HARVEY. Bell Berkeley, do not charge all to me. Remember your promise made on the bloody field of Ball's Bluff. Lieutenant take from my pocket my letter of instructions signed by this woman. [*Lieutenant takes order and reads it.*]

LIEUT. I see by this that you are responsible for the cruel treatment this poor soldier has received. [*Converses apart with soldiers.*]

BELL. [*Aside.*] Curse that order! I see that the fates are against me.

HARRY. Where am I? Where is the old flag? Sergeant Harvey where is the bread I earned by bowing to Bell Berkeley? Ah, I remember all; your Harvey has won your hand by cruel, cruel treatment to me for the last three years. You will soon be happy, and I—father why do you not come? I must have something to eat! I will never bow to Bell Berkeley! [*Sees flag.*] The dear, dear old flag! It has been a long, long time since I saw it! Boys let us give three loud cheers——[*Falls back with maniacal laugh.*]

SOLDIER. Lieutenant, let us bear him away from this accursed spot. He is crazy.

HARRY. Sergeant Harvey, don't kick me! I will beg your pardon! Tell Bell Berkeley—[*is assisted to his feet.*] Boys—[*discovers Bell and Harvey*] drive them off! They come to punish us! They will not give us bread! Devils! Fiends!! Why do you thus torture me? In the name of Heaven leave me! Bell Berkeley, there stands your husband, who gained your hand by the cruel treatment I received daily from him by your orders.

LIEUT. Boys, take that rebel sergeant and bind him to a post in the sight of bread for two weeks, and once a day give him barely enough to keep body and soul together. [*Guard with Harvey exit R.*] This noted female spy and fiend I will report to General Devans.

BELL. Yes Lieutenant, Harry Bacon has received punishment at my hands for which I am not sorry.

LIEUT. Aren't you ashamed?

BELL. By the memory of my murdered father and brother I would do it over.

LIEUT. [*Draws revolver.*] Your life shall be the forfeit. [*His arm is stayed by Harry.*]

HARRY. No, Lieutenant, remember she is a woman. We did not enter the army to wage war upon women.

BELL. [*Defiantly.*] Fire, miscreant! Harry Bacon, I do not thank you for your interference.

HARRY. My sainted mother would not approve of an act where life is the forfeit. Do you think your mother would?

BELL. [*Stage illuminates and Mrs. Berkeley appears at back as an angel.*] Oh, mother, mother, my poor mother. [*Kneels toward mother in tableau.*]

SCENE V.

FULL STAGE.—*Surrender of Confederate Forces, and Columbia hands bugle toward Union soldiers. Heavy light, slow curtain.*

END OF ACT IV.

ACT V. SCENE I.

PARLOR—*John Bacon's. Place, Loudon county, Va. Time, April 24, 1865. John B., C.; Jane B., L. C.; Capt. Sam'l H., U. L.; Uncle Pete, extreme L.; Mary W., R. C.; two chairs extreme R.; table in center of room.*

JOHN B. Since the surrender of General Lee, we have been unable to hear from Harry. Had he been alive after the evacuation of Richmond I am sure he would have written. Uncle Pete you will go once more to the office.

PETE. Yes sah, I'd run fru fire fo' dat boy, and now I's jist gwine.
[*Exit L.*]

SAM. H. I feel confident, although the authorities did not accept Generals Johnston and Sherman's agreement, that Johnston will surrender upon any terms. Kirby Smith will follow in his wake, then this cruel war will be over.

JANE B. I know many a mother, wife and sister will only be too glad for the termination of this war. Think what the suffering and anguish will be to those who gave their all for their country. The poor mother expecting to meet an only son ; the wife her husband ; the sister her brother ; the children a loved father, and we today living in hopes of meeting a loved son and brother, only to have our hopes blasted by his non-arrival. Oh, disappointment thou hast sunk the hearts of millions ! [*Wringing hands.*]

MARY W. I received a letter from Charles who wrote from Washington yesterday, he does not even mention Harry's name.

SAM'L. H. Ladies, I do not see the necessity of borrowing trouble. No doubt he is sick or delayed. He'll report soon.

PETE. [*Enter L. with letter.*] Massa Bacon here's a letter from dat boy, I know'd it was from Harry by de nice writin' on de wrapper. [*Jane tries to take it.*] You go 'long, dis letter is from Massa Bacon.
[*Hands letter*]

JANE B. Uncle Pete you act so meanly lately that I don't know what to do.

PETE. I'll tell you, walk right up to Massa Hansford and kiss 'im.

JANE B. [*Boxing his ears*]. Take that for your impudence.

JOHN B. This letter *is* from Harry, I'll read what the dear boy says :

WASHINGTON, D. C., April 23, 1865.

To FATHER, SISTER AND ALL MY DEAR FRIENDS:

I have been quite recently liberated from Belle Island, where I had been held in solitary confinement by Bell Berkeley and her coadjutor, John Harvey. I had orders from the Secretary of War to report in person at his office as soon as I was able to go. I reported this morning and was handed a furlough and a Captain's commission in the United States Army. No doubt I'll give this letter a chase, as I shall leave on the express, and stop of at Point off Rocks.

My love to all,

HARRY.

PETE. Read de P. S.

JOHN B. There is no P. S.

PETE. I knows dere is a P. S. De P is positive and de S is sure, so we is positive and sure dat Massa Harry 'll be here. [*yawns*.]

[*Knocking L.*]

JANE B. Uncle Pete go to the door. Harry is there !

PETE. [*Jumping up.*] Is dat so? I'd run fru fire fur dat boy. [*Goes to door L.*] Walk in, walk right in Massa Harry. [*Enter Harry as Capt. U. S. A., and Chas. Wilford as 1st Lieut. Vols. General hand shaking, and seats.*]

JOHN B. Well my boy, I just received your letter.

HARRY. I am glad you did. It is the first letter I have written for over three years. I am glad to meet so many of my friends here this evening. Captain, how is the old command ?

SAM. H. You would not be at home there now. But a very few of the original number left. It is over three years since you fell into Bell's—

HARRY. Please Captain, never refer to my captivity. I have suffered much at her hands. I do not wish to live over it again. I wish by associations with my friends for the three months I remain at home, to banish from my mind that I had ever been a prisoner of war. Had I been treated as other prisoners I would not care, but by being kept in solitary confinement, and the abuse I received daily almost racked my reason.

MARY. Let us do all in our power to entertain these boys, and make them happy! Bell's property has been confiscated since her mother's death.

HARRY. Is her mother dead?

MARY. She died last March one year ago. After hearing of Bell's matrimonial alliance with John Harvey, she pined away until death came to her relief. Uncle Pete told us all about her actions at Ball's Bluff and Mrs. Berkeley learned it from the servants.

JOHN B. Mrs. Berkeley was an excellent woman, I firmly believe that she was true to the Union, but through fear, and having lost her husband and only son in the war she dared not express herself. I have lost much in property and mourned for an only son, and today I feel like rejoicing for his safe return. Harry, your three years captivity will only make you love your country and friends more. We can only thank him "who presides over the destinies of men" for your safe return Girls sing "Home again." (*Mary and Jane sings the song entitled, "Home again.*")

HARRY. I feel as if all my suffering was not in vain. There is much however, to be done for the poor freedmen.

PETE. Massa Harry, I's no more de bone of 'cession. I's a free darky eber since I's gwine and cooked de and-so-forth.

JOHN B. Uncle Pete you are free. Virtually you were free when the late lamented President Lincoln issued his immancipation proclamation. It only remains to be seen what you can do for yourself.

PETE. (*Jumping on chair.*) Dis is what I's gwine for to do, I's gwine for to make a speech. Feller citizens: (*gesticulating.*) I's jist gwine for to rise and compound de African question ob abolition slavery. I's gwine for to place before de dark grim visage ob de white man dat de nigger—*dat de nigger*—DAT DE NIGGER—yes feller citizens dat is what I's gwine for to do. (*Sits.*)

JANE B. Why Uncle Pete you are quite an orator.

PETE. I's gwine for to be a senator !

JOHN B. There are no doubt some freedman who may become senators.

PETE. I's made up my mind to play a bold game of Bluff.

SAM'L H. What, Ball's Bluff?

PETE. (*Laughing.*) You go 'long, what does yer know about cards ? When dat Bell Berkeley—(*knocking L.*)

JOHN B. Uncle Pete go to the door.

PETE. Yes sah ! I's jist gwine for to go, but as I said when dat Bell—

HARRY. Did you hear what father said ?

PETE. Yes sah, but as I said before when dat Bell Berkeley——

JOHN. B. Jane go to the door.

PETE. (*Rising and going to door L.*) Its berry funny I can't tell what dat Bell Berkeley——(*Staggers back to C.*)

JOHN B. Uncle Pete, what is the matter ?

PETE. (*Pointing to Bell B. who advances C, clad in deep mourning.*) Dat woman has de imperdence of de debil.

JOHN B. What brings you here ?

JANE B. Bell Berkeley why do you heep insult upon injury ? Why have you dared to cross this threshold where you have caused so much misery ? Look upon my brother and ask yourself the question, whether you have not had sufficient revenge? If God can forgive you I can not!

MARY W. Nor. I Yes look upon Harry Bacon and ask yourself why you ordered that poor miserable tool—John Harvey—to starve and otherwise abuse a soldier of the United States? Bell Berkeley, once beloved by us all, in the name of Heaven, after practicing your fiendish tortures upon him (*Pointing to Harry.*) Why do you impose yourself here?

JOHN B. Bell Berkeley, I will tell you why you are here. You are here to witness something for which I long have wished. (*Walking L, with Jane.*) Captain Hansford I wish to speak to you. (*Hansford goes L. to Jane B.*) I long have watched my daughter and know that her happiness is only complete in your keeping. (*Unites their hands.*) Daughter, you have a father's blessing. (*Walks to Mary and leads her R. C.*) Mary, I can never forget the interest you have taken in the welfare of my only son. Harry step this way. (*Harry goes R.*)

BELL. (*Moves C. aside.*) And is it for this I am here?

JOHN B. Harry, you have suffered much. Your cup of misery has been constantly overflowing for the past three years. That fiend has——

HARRY. Please father, do not refer to her.

BELL. Let him go, I deserve all he may say. But to witness this is more than I can bear!

PETE. Why in de debil don't yer git dat rebel Harvey and hab a weddin' ob your own?

CHAS. W. Uncle Pete, you must keep quiet.

PETE. I's quiet, but who's gwine for to shut dere mouf when she's here.

JOHN B. Mary, may your devotion to my son be of such a nature that he will forget the suffering he has endured during his captivity. Harry remember you are a Bacon! Cherish and protect Mary and you will be happy. [*Joins hands.*] Bell Berkeley, for this happy reunion you came to witness.

PETE. Dat's what I say. I's been to de war too. Can't you gib me a wife? Gib me dat Bell Berkeley, I'll make a 'missive wife outen her.

BELL. Mr. Bacon, I have erred and sinnedagainst God and man. My pride, my silly pride, kept me up. What I did, I did through fancied wrongs. Many a time when the angry passions had subsided, I tried to think about my past life. Through the death of my father and brother, and goaded on by John Harvey, I became a fiend; and through the instructions of satan I performed deeds that hell itself might be ashamed of. Through my actions I am a poor outcast, not having a place to call my own. Oh, Mr. Bacon, [*falling on her knees*] do not be too severe with me now. I freely confess that I have been guilty of torturing and starving Harry—that I am suffering the torments of the damned. When the first step downward is taken, the second naturally follows. I am so steeped in crime that Heaven has forever shut its Golden Gates upon me. I am forever lost! Oh, Mr. Bacon, have you not one kind word for me? I see that you can not forgive me for the misery I wantonly caused! [*Kneeling to Harry.*] Oh, Harry, can you not have one kind word for me after acknowledging what I have, and kneeling voluntarily to you, not as you had to do when forced by stavation and abuse? Can you not forgive me and let me be a wanderer over

creation's face free of you at least. Your haggard face has haunted me
nightly, for the past two years. But that fiend, John Harvey, aided by
satan, goaded me on and made me what you have so justly called me.
Oh, Harry, why do you not speak to me? Are you now fulfilling your
part by calling to memory what you told my father four years ago, on
the afternoon of that fatal quarrel? You said then, "beware that your
curses may not fall upon your head and yours." Oh, Harry, have we
not in common suffered? Have I not said enough to move you to pity?

HARRY. Bell Berkely, I have suffered much at your hands. You
and John Harvey almost destroyed my reason. You not only made me
suffer, but those who are near and dear to me. I can never forget that
you, once a friend, did this. I will not be too severe. If our friends
can forgive, I will try. [*Turning to audience.*] Friends, can you forgive her?

[*Picture—Stage illuminates, and Mrs. Berkeley and Mrs. Bacon appear
at back as angel. Slow Curtain. Soft Music. Curtain.*

THE END.